Through a Different Lens

Through a Different Lens

Revealing the
Transformative and Spiritual Power
in Movies

Carmen Leal

THE
PILGRIM
PRESS
Cleveland

For Gary, who watched hundreds of movies with me, helping me whittle my list to nine perfect choices and patiently listening to every synopsis, every chapter outline, and every other detail during our morning mile.

For all the Christians in Hollywood in front of and behind the camera who strive to use this exciting medium to be a light in an increasingly dark world.!U

The Pilgrim Press
700 Prospect Avenue
Cleveland, Ohio 44115-1100
thepilgrimpress.com

Copyright © 2013 by Carmen Scott

No part of this publication may be stored in a retrieval system, or transmitted in any form or by any means, electronic, mechanical, photocopying, recording, or otherwise (brief quotations used in magazines or newspaper reviews excepted), without the prior permission of the publisher.

All right reserved. Published in 2013

Printed in the United States of America

Library of Congress Cataloging-in-Publication Data
Leal, Carmen, 1954–
    Through a different lens : revealing the transformative and spiritual power in movies / Carmen Leal.
      pages   cm
    ISBN 978-0-8298-1973-1 (alk. paper)
    1. Bible – In motion pictures. 2. Religion in motion pictures.
3. Motion pictures – Religious aspects. I. Title.
PN1995.9.R4L43   2013
791.43'6822 – dc23
2013033217

                1 2 3 4 5 6 7 8 9

People become really quite remarkable when they start thinking that they can do things. When they believe in themselves they have the first secret of success.
—Norman Vincent Peale

We do not believe in ourselves until someone reveals that deep inside us something is valuable, worth listening to, worthy of our trust, sacred to our touch. Once we believe in ourselves we can risk curiosity, wonder, spontaneous delight, or any experience.
—e e cummings

Contents

Preface   ix
Introduction   1
Movie Themes   5
Christian Symbols in Movies   9
How to Use This Book   11
Copyright Protection   15

One	The Transformative Power of Potential *The Wizard of Oz*	17
Two	The Transformative Power of Purpose *Hugo*	31
Three	The Transformative Power of Priorities *Mr. Holland's Opus*	44
Four	The Transformative Power of Prayer *Lilies of the Field*	57
Five	The Transformative Power of Practice *Akeelah and the Bee*	72
Six	The Transformative Power of Perseverance *Under the Same Moon*	86
Seven	The Transformative Power of Pain *We Are Marshall*	100
Eight	The Transformative Power of Pardon *The Harimaya Bridge*	113
Nine	The Transformative Power of the Prize *Rudy*	128

Final Comments   143
Credits   145

Preface

In 2000 I attended the Colorado Christian Writers Conference in Estes Park, Colorado, and heard a keynote speech by Barbara Nicolosi, the founder and executive director of Act One: Writing for Hollywood. In her talk she told us that if we were Christians and we were writers and we were not writing for Hollywood then we did not deserve to complain about Hollywood. She went on to say that if we were Christians and not praying for Hollywood then, once again, we did not have the right to complain about the movies in our theaters.

I can still remember sitting there thinking that she had come all the way from California, and I from Florida, so I could hear that exact message at that exact time. It was one of those pivotal moments in my life.

I attended a weekend screenwriting retreat that fall followed by an intensive five-week program the following summer. I had hopes of writing an award-winning screenplay and using my words to make a difference. I attended those events because Barbara and others believed in me. I could look at the years that have followed as being a failure, as my screenplay remains unfinished at draft number ten, and I have no film credits to my name.

Life happened, and while my screenplay is unfinished, my passion for using movies as a starting point for theological discussions has never burned brighter. Over the years I've spoken to large and small groups both inside and outside church settings and shared my love of movies and how to look at them from the perspective of a Christian worldview. The lessons I learned through Act One, the people I met, the discussions I shared have all prepared me to write this book for you.

Learning takes place in many ways. I believe the most effective and longest lasting is through stories, and, after Jesus, no one tells stories better than Hollywood. In my summer class I was privileged to learn from Christian writers, directors, producers, agents, and actors with names and credits you would instantly recognize. One statement they all made in different ways was that there is not so much a bias against Christians in Hollywood as much as there is a bias against bad art—or bad art that doesn't make money.

As you read this book and discuss the movies and apply them to your lives, please remember to pray for Hollywood as an industry and specifically for the Christians who are trying to make good art that makes money and, more importantly, a difference.

I hope *Through a Different Lens* will encourage you to look at movies in a new way while helping you to believe in yourself and others. Most of all I hope this book brings you closer to God and to understanding that God never wastes anything. God made you to be the person you are with your unique gifts and abilities, and now it's up to you to figure out how to use them.

Grab some popcorn, watch some movies, and make a difference.

Introduction

We tend to get what we expect.
—Norman Vincent Peale

In the summer of 1992 *Sister Act* hit theaters in a big way. Touchstone Pictures probably figured that with Academy Award winning actress Whoopi Goldberg in the starring role they would break even, or have a modest hit. No one expected that the opening weekend box office revenue of almost $12 million would grow to a worldwide gross of $26.6 million. With little marketing or fanfare, *Sister Act* became what is known as a sleeper, or a surprise hit, growing in popularity over time through word-of-mouth marketing.

In the first few lines of the film a nun calls on the young Dolores to name all the apostles. Obviously the class clown, Dolores answers, "John, Paul, George... and Ringo!"

"Dolores Wilson," snaps the exasperated teacher. "You are the most unruly, disobedient girl in this school! Now, I want you to march right up to that blackboard and write the names of all the apostles alphabetically."

Dolores swaggers to the blackboard and writes, "John, Paul, Peter..., and Elvis."

Frustrated, the nun yells, "This is enough! You are hopeless, and I wash my hands of you. Mark my words, Dolores. If you continue on this disruptive track, it will lead straight to the devil. Have you any idea what girls like you become?" We see that the nun's words become a prophecy when the next scene cuts to the now adult Dolores belting out standards in a low-budget nightclub.

I remember sitting in the dark theater thinking how like the young Dolores I was when I attended Holy Name Elementary School. I too was the class clown, and while I probably would not have ended up as a lounge singer like Whoopi Goldberg's character, my life might have turned out vastly different had it not been for one person who believed in me. However, it wasn't until more than thirty-five years later that I met that person.

When my father died, my family made the trek to Kansas for his funeral. During the luncheon held in the school cafeteria a woman approached me and introduced herself as the mother of one of my fourth-grade classmates.

After sharing her condolences, she told me that it was at her suggestion that I was moved from the fourth to the eighth grade English class. She had seen first hand my antics and disruptive behavior and, thankfully, looked beyond that to see whom I could become if my intelligence, humor, and energy were focused in other directions. Without my or my parents' knowledge, as room mother she argued with my teacher and the principal about the merits of challenging me in a subject I loved. I soon moved to the Junior Great Books program, where we read the classics. I can still remember how hard I had to work to keep up with the older kids. When I finished classroom work in other subjects I'd read one of my books instead of getting into trouble.

"I knew you weren't a bad child," she explained, "but I also knew that if you weren't challenged you would never realize your potential. I talked to your teacher, and that's why you went to the eighth grade English class that year."

"Then I'm the one who needs to thank you," I interrupted

"Lucien bragged about all of you children," she continued, bushing off my thanks. "Because I had a connection, whenever I'd see your father I'd ask about you. Your father told me about your being an exchange student in Brazil and about those two years in the Peace Corps in Africa. He talked about your music and your children, but he talked most about your books. He was so proud."

My parents were both readers and encouraged all of us in that direction. It was during that year in the Junior Great Books program, however, when my love affair with reading began. I remember being enthralled with the stories. The Junior Great

Books program introduced me to wonderful stories and set my feet on the path to becoming a storyteller. This room mother, who had remained anonymous for so long, believed in me and changed the course of my life even when I didn't know it.

I had never known why I had been moved to the other class for an hour each day, or that my friend's mother had seen something in me, but I am grateful. I don't remember her at all. In fact I can't even remember having room mothers. I was humbled and honored that she took the time to come to my father's funeral and to share what happened in fourth grade. It wasn't the first time someone believed in me, but I can tell you it helped to create who I am today and all I have achieved.

One story I remember from that pivotal year is *Pygmalion* by George Bernard Shaw. I was excited when that fall *My Fair Lady* starring Audrey Hepburn opened in our town. My father filled our station wagon with my siblings and me and assorted neighborhood kids and headed for the drive-in. Most of us ran to the play area for the duration of the nearly three-hour movie, but not me. I watched the entire film and to this day it remains one of my favorite musicals and is, in fact, the inspiration for this book.

In *My Fair Lady*, a retelling of *Pygmalion*, Eliza Dolittle is transformed from a flower girl to a lady. At the end of the movie she explains to Professor Higgins's mother that while her son gave her elocution lessons and dressed her in the appropriate attire, it was Colonel Pickering who taught her to behave as a lady.

"You see, Mrs. Higgins, apart from the things one can pick up, the difference between a lady and a flower girl is not how she behaves but how she is treated. I shall always be a flower girl to Professor Higgins... because he always treats me as a flower girl and always will. But I know I shall always be a lady to Colonel Pickering... because he always treats me as a lady and always will."

I call what she describes the Pygmalion Principle, and it's really quite simple. From Eliza we learn that we need to believe in ourselves and to believe in others. I'd like to add one more principle, and that is that we must accept that God believes in us. In fact, God believed in us before we were born, and he will never stop believing in us. He believes in us enough to transform us from sinner to saint through his son and to reach our full potential.

When we believe in others, even when no one else does, people are transformed. We have to believe in others and ourselves if we are to use our gifts and talents for our God-ordained purpose. Hollywood is filled with stories where someone believed when it wasn't popular or, on the surface, didn't make sense. There are movies where those who believed did so in private, like my fourth-grade champion, or like my father, they shouted their belief for the world to hear.

Through a Different Lens takes a look at nine principles that we all need to live by if we are to live full lives in Christ—though there are many others we could also discuss. Each chapter is based on a movie where a character believes something will happen against all odds and, because of that character's belief, or the belief of others, the goal is achieved.

The hardest part of writing this book has been choosing only nine movies. Dozens of movies were screened for each chapter and set aside even though they were great movies. Some movies that did not make the cut, like *Erin Brockovich*, feature real people and as such I share their stories as examples. I wanted movies from different generations with flawed characters who exhibit growth beyond simply achieving a goal. I chose to include films from different genres with a wide variety of interesting situations.

While there are many excellent R movies (*"Restricted. Children under 17 require accompanying parent or adult guardian"*) that fit the chapter themes I have chosen to use only movies rated PG or PG-13 for this book.

These are not the best movies ever made, though I would argue a couple fit that description. I hope you enjoy applying these principles to your own life and, hopefully, begin looking at movies through a different lens.

Movie Themes

There are countless screenwriting books that discuss themes and plots. Some say there are a set number of plots in literature (books and movies) and that number, depending upon the author or teacher, ranges from one to thirty-six. The reality is that there is one plot: the hero wants to do or have something he or she doesn't have when the movie begins. The rest of the movie is a story detailing the successful or not so successful journey to get what he or she wants.

Plot twists are what make movies entertaining and unique, and those are dictated by the themes. Any good movie has conflict, characters we love and characters we love to hate. In choosing movies to feature in *Through a Different Lens*, I focused on those that have a strong emphasis on the main characters believing in themselves and/or others believing in them. Each movie has several themes that enrich the plot and add layers of complexity. These are not new themes. In fact, every theme is found in the Bible over and over.

That's not so very different from our personal life story on a spiritual level. Heaven is our real home. Some of us figure that out at a very young age; some never do. The rest of our life is living through those plot twists and turns as we make our way to our final home. Along the way we may lose our belief in ourselves to carry on, and someone is there to lift us up. Other times there is nothing we can't do, and we use that energy to help others.

The Internet has a plethora of sites featuring movie plots and themes. Here is a list of ten themes that should be familiar since they are the basis for the vast majority of stories both in books and on screen:

MOVIE THEMES

Death as a Part of Life	Humans as Spiritual Beings
Good vs. Evil	People vs. Themselves
Individual vs. Society	Humans vs. Nature
Loss of Innocence	Revenge
Love Conquers All	Triumph over Adversity

Each of the featured movies fits into one or more of the themes, and you'll also find subthemes to discuss. You may have different ideas about each movie's major theme. There are no right or wrong answers and the list is not comprehensive, just another way to get us thinking and discussing.

Wizard of Oz (Humans vs. Themselves)

Compassion	Potential in Self and Others
Courage	Running Away from Problems
Finding Home	The Prodigal
Personal Growth	Wisdom

Hugo (Triumph over Adversity)

Brokenness	Personal Growth
Family	Purpose
Finding Home	Redemption

Mr. Holland's Opus (Love Conquers All)

Family	Priorities
Fidelity	Self-Sacrifice
Passion	Servanthood

Lilies of the Field (Humans as Spiritual Beings)

Community	Prayer
Foundations	Pride
God's Will	Trust

MOVIE THEMES

Akeelah and the Bee (Triumph over Adversity)
Community	Goals
Discipline	Practice
Gifts	Failure

Under the Same Moon (Love Conquers All)
Family	Love
Illegal Immigration	Perseverance
Kindness	Sacrifice

We Are Marshall (Death as a Part of Life)
Adversity	Pain
Grief	Restoration
Hope	Starting Over

The Harimaya Bridge (Revenge)
Anger	Pardon
Grief	Pride
Pain	Starting Over

Rudy (Humans vs. Themselves)
Affirmation	Friendship
Courage	Hope
Determination	The Prize

Christian Symbols in Movies: The Wizard of Oz

Frank L. Baum always said that his *Oz* books did not have any hidden spiritual themes. He set out to write, as he put it, an all-American fairy tale to rival those of Europe. We will never know for sure if that was his singular goal, but generations have been delighted by the stories and many of them have found spiritual themes in them.

I looked at *The Wizard of Oz* for the umpteenth time while choosing movies for this book. This time, however, I put on my Christian worldview glasses and discovered several undeniably Christian themes. Take a look at the themes list and see how many of them apply to *The Wizard of Oz*. Depending upon which character's point of view, all of them are represented. If we dig deeper we can find some profoundly Christian symbols sprinkled throughout the movie.

Good versus Evil

The most obvious of Christian themes is the battle between good and evil represented by Glinda the Good Witch and the Wicked Witch of the West. I am sure God has had conversations with Satan similar to the one Glinda had with the Wicked Witch when she said, "Oh, rubbish. You have no power here. Be gone, before someone drops a house on you, too."

The Yellow Brick Road

The next symbol even comes with its own song. The Yellow Brick Road is God's path to righteousness. When Glinda told Dorothy that if she stayed on the path that nothing would harm her, she believed the Good Witch. We would do well to heed God's word when it comes to staying on the path as we go through life.

Ruby Red Slippers

After Glinda foiled the Wicked Witch's plan to claim the prize, Glinda told Dorothy, "Remember, never let those ruby slippers off your feet for a moment, or you will be at the mercy of the Wicked Witch of the West." The Ruby Red Slippers are symbols of the tremendous power of obedience. The power Dorothy wore on her feet represented the power we all have when we trust and obey God and choose to live not only for today but for eternity. Of course the Wicked Witch wanted those slippers so badly she was willing to kill for them. When we wear our spiritual ruby slippers we incur the wrath and jealously of the enemy. By staying on the Yellow Brick Road God keeps us safe.

Over the Rainbow

Can you imagine *The Wizard of Oz* without Dorothy singing "Over the Rainbow"? It very nearly happened when, after a screening, the powers that be felt the song slowed down the action, and it was almost cut. Thankfully they kept the song, and we got to hear Dorothy sing about her longing for a way to fly over the rainbow where there were no problems. Doesn't that sound like heaven?

As you watch the movies and begin to study them you'll be amazed at the Christian symbols you will find in each movie.

How to Use This Book

> *Therefore, do not throw away*
> *your confidence, which has a great reward.*
> *For you have need of endurance,*
> *so that when you have done the will of God,*
> *you may receive what was promised.*
> —HEBREWS 10:35–36

In the 1991 movie *Grand Canyon*, Steve Martin, in the role of Davis, says, "You know what your problem is, it's that you haven't seen enough movies—all of life's riddles are answered in the movies." I don't believe that the answers to all of life's riddles are in the movies, but as a former educator, trainer, and professional speaker, I am convinced that we learn from hearing stories that strike a chord within us.

Stories that come from everyday life, like the parables that Jesus told, transform our perspectives. Movies are not only cinematic storytelling on a universal level, but they often provide valuable lessons in the process. The lessons we learn through movies and other stories can change us. Movies can teach while touching, inspire while delighting. They can motivate and challenge us and put our feet on a new path. In short, movies can be transformative. *Through a Different Lens* is a resource that can be used in Sunday school, small group studies, youth groups, and individual study.

Recognizing that many church Sunday schools take a summer hiatus, there are nine chapters, one for each month of a traditional academic year. Because the chapters do not build on each other as in a traditional Bible study they can be studied in any order and at any pace.

The featured movies can be watched in a group setting, such as during a church movie night, or as a small group or youth activity. They can also be watched individually. All the movies are available to rent through NetFlix.com, Blockbuster.

com, Hulu.com, and other online resources. They can be purchased from Blockbuster.com and Amazon.com or at brick and mortar locations. They can often be borrowed for a small fee or even for free at your local library.

If your Sunday school or small group is using this as a study, it is helpful to have a group leader. Everything needed to lead the discussion is included. If you choose to take this route it is a good idea for group leaders to watch the movie in its entirety ahead of time even if they have seen it before.

I have chosen not to feature selected clip suggestions for each movie to show during the class. Many churches do not have access to the appropriate audiovisual equipment, which makes it difficult to show specific clips. The average Sunday school class, youth group, or small group often limits the discussion to one hour or less. The detailed synopsis, even for those who have not seen the movie before or in a long time, can help participants follow the discussion.

Using the Discussion Guide

Each chapter includes a four-week study guide to use during a month of Sunday school or small group sessions. If your group prefers a one-week discussion format, please use the four weeks as a menu and create your own personal study guide.

Once you or your group have watched the movie, the examples and questions will help move the after-movie conversation from the story to a deeper spiritual life-application discussion. The group leader may use the chapter contents as a teaching tool. Participants will want their own copy for study before or after viewing and/or group discussions. Each chapter includes the following sections:

Synopsis

A movie synopsis to help refresh our memory of key movie moments, characters, and plot turns, and thought-provoking scriptures, quotes, and questions to aid participants to apply these principles.

HOW TO USE THIS BOOK 13

Principle Scriptures
This is in no way an exhaustive theological dissertation. It is, instead, a way to jumpstart a lively, focused discussion. Each movie discussion guide draws on spiritual themes with life-application.

Principle Ponderings
Principle Ponderings, a series of questions taken from the movie plot, add another layer to the biblical and life-application discussion.

Principle Philosophies
These short bursts of spiritual truisms are designed to give readers the opportunity to focus on specific areas in their physical and spiritual lives.

Principle Passages
Thought-provoking quotations help participants to look deeper into each movie theme.

Principle Possibilities
These questions allow group members to explore deeper meanings in the movies rather than accepting them as simply entertainment. The questions are a call to action to those wishing to apply the lessons learned to their own lives. This section of the guide can be used to create a group dialogue or for personal at-home study.

Principle Point ৩৯
Trivia surrounding the making of each movie are included in each guide.

At the end of the fourth week study guides are stories about well-known persons and how they applied the chapter principles to their lives

Copyright Protection

It's important to know and understand the copyright laws governing viewing movies in a public place. Many if not most people believe that if they buy or rent a copy of a movie they may show that movie to as many people as they choose in any location. The following explanation of U.S. Copyright Law is presented to educate you so that no one unintentionally breaks the law while enjoying the movies featured in this book.

The Federal Copyright Act (Title 17 of the U.S. Code) governs how copyrighted materials, such as movies, may be used. When you buy or rent a movie you are allowed to show it in your own home exclusively unless the location where you choose to view the movie is licensed for public exhibition. This legal copyright compliance requirement applies to churches and schools as well as any other public location whether you are charging an admission fee or not. It also applies even if you got a copy of the movie off the Internet or through a streaming site such as Netflix, Blockbuster.com, or Hulu.com.

If your small group or youth group chooses to watch movies together in a private home, then you will not require a license. If, however, your church or group has a movie night at church or another public location, then you will need a license.

Obtaining a public performance license is easy and affordable. Your church or your denomination may already be licensed, so you'll want to check first before buying a duplicate license. If there is no license in place you can get an umbrella license from the Motion Picture Licensing Corporation by calling 800-462-8855 or visiting www.mplc.com. Be sure to mention your church affiliation and they may refer you to Christian Video Licensing International at 888-771-2854. You may also visit them at www.cvli.org for more information.

—ONE—

Principle Scripture
Now to him who is able to do immeasurably more than all we ask or imagine, according to his power that is at work within us.
—Ephesians 3:20

The Transformative Power of
POTENTIAL

The Wizard of Oz

RUN YOUR OWN RACE

You can if you think you can.
—Norman Vincent Peale

Comparing ourselves to others is common at all ages, but never more so than with teenagers who have yet to discover their potential. Imagine your acting debut when your father is Danny Thomas, one of the country's biggest television stars. That's exactly what seventeen-year-old Marlo Thomas faced one summer while preparing for her first lead role at a local playhouse. Her pride at appearing on stage soon turned to fear when all the interviewers questioned her abilities when compared to her legendary father.

The young thespian told her father that she was so worried she wanted to change her name. Instead of being angry her father gave her the perfect answer and a life lesson. "I raised you to be a thoroughbred. When thoroughbreds run they wear blinders to keep their eyes focused straight ahead with no distractions, no other horses. They hear the crowd, but they don't listen. They just run their own race. That's what you have to do. Don't listen to anyone comparing you to me or to anyone else. You just run your own race."

On opening night, with renewed excitement because of her father's words, she received a package backstage. Inside was a pair of old horse blinders with a little note that read, "Run your own race, Baby." With a few words and a pair of old horse blinders, Danny Thomas told his daughter that she needed to focus on her own potential and not compare herself to anyone else.

In *The Wizard of Oz,* Dorothy has to run a race too. It would have been easy for her to go off course like horses without blinders, but by staying on the Yellow Brick Road she was able to discover that the potential to go home was always within her. The same can be said for her three cohorts, who doubted their own potential.

After running her summer stock race Marlo appeared on a number of television shows and finally showed her true potential in *That Girl* and a number of movies that garnered her critical acclaim and awards.

Like Dorothy and Marlo, we have to put on blinders to follow our own road and discover our potential, blinders that allow us to be in the world, not of the world. Part of that potential lies in learning the importance of seeing beyond our sinful nature and flaws to become the person God created us to be.

Let's go "Over the Rainbow"

po•ten•tial. *noun.* **The inherent ability or capacity for growth, development, or coming into being**

According to Anne Frank, "Everyone has inside of him a piece of good news. The good news is that you don't know how great you can be! How much you can love! What you can accomplish! And what your potential is!" This chapter looks at the importance of seeing beyond our sinful nature and flaws to become the person God created us to be.

THE WIZARD OF OZ

Synopsis

Newspaperman Rick Polito of the *Marin Independent* wrote a now-famous one-sentence television listing for *The Wizard of Oz*. "Transported to a surreal landscape, a young girl kills the first person she meets and then teams up with three strangers to kill again." While one could say that happened, it's not the complete story. That started with an orphaned teenager growing up on a Kansas farm.

Dorothy Gale (Judy Garland) lives with her Auntie Em and Uncle Henry. After being provoked, Dorothy's beloved dog, Toto, bites Almirah Gulch (Margaret Hamilton). Miss Gulch owns half the county and convinces the sheriff to give her an order to have the "dangerous" dog destroyed. Dorothy begs her aunt and uncle to disregard the order, but being law-abiding citizens they tell Dorothy she must give Toto to Miss Gulch.

As Miss Gulch rides away on her bicycle with the dog in a rear basket, Toto jumps out and runs home. Dorothy realizes Miss Gulch will come back when she finds out that Toto has escaped, so she decides to run away. On her journey Dorothy meets Professor Marvel (Frank Morgan) a fortune-teller and balloonist who tricks Dorothy into believing her Auntie Em has suffered an attack of some sort because Dorothy has run away. Dorothy rushes home in a panic. An approaching cyclone delays her, and, by the time she gets home, her aunt and uncle and three farmhands are in the storm cellar.

When she can't open the cellar door, she goes inside the house and into her bedroom, where she is knocked unconscious by a window hitting her on the head. She comes to and realizes that the house is inside the cyclone. Through the window Dorothy sees Miss Gulch, first riding on her bicycle, then transformed into a witch on a broomstick. With a thud the house lands in Munchkinland, a section of Oz filled with little people, and falls on top of the Wicked Witch of the East, killing her instantly.

The Munchkins thank her for doing away with the witch. From a ball of light in the sky Glinda the Good Witch of the North (Billie Burke) appears confused as to whether Dorothy is a good witch or a bad witch. The Wicked Witch of the West arrives and tries to remove the magic ruby red slippers from the dead witch, but Glinda moves first and places them on Dorothy's feet. Glinda cautions Dorothy to never remove the slippers because, as long as she wears them, she will be safe. The Wicked Witch of the West leaves in a fury, vowing to get revenge on Dorothy for killing her sister.

Dorothy insists she wants to go home to Kansas, so Glinda tells her she needs to talk to the Wizard of Oz, who lives in the Emerald City. When Dorothy asks how she can find the Emerald City Glinda tells her to "follow the Yellow Brick Road." On the road she meets a talking scarecrow (Ray Bolger,) a tin man (Jack Haley,) and a cowardly lion (Bert Lahr.) When Dorothy learns that each of her traveling companions wants something special, she suggests they come with her down the Yellow Brick Road. She is convinced that if the Wizard of Oz can get her home to Kansas, he can give the scarecrow a brain, the tin man a heart, and the lion courage.

On the way to the Emerald City, the Wicked Witch tries to derail their plans, but Glinda uses her good magic to protect them. At first the great Wizard won't see them, but, thanks to the doorkeeper, they finally get into the palace. The Wizard won't help them, until they bring him the broomstick of the Wicked Witch of the West.

The four of them plus Toto head to the castle to retrieve the broom, but the witch sends winged monkeys to attack them, and Dorothy and Toto are captured. When the witch discovers that the Ruby Slippers can't be taken as long as Dorothy is alive, she turns her hourglass and threatens to kill Dorothy when the sand runs out. With the help of her friends Dorothy almost escapes, but the witch sets the Scarecrow on fire. Dorothy douses him with a pail of water, splashing the witch and causing her to melt. The guards, happy that the tyrannical witch is dead, give Dorothy the broomstick and they return to the Emerald City.

Once they show the broom to the guard, they are given an audience with the Wizard. Toto pulls aside a curtain to reveal an old man pulling levers and speaking into a microphone. The Wizard is apologetic and helps Dorothy's companions realize that they already had what they sought. He bestows gifts on them: a diploma for the Scarecrow, a medal of valor for the Lion, and a huge heart-shaped watch for the Tin Man. When Dorothy asks about going home to Kansas, the Wizard suggests that he take her in his hot-air balloon. Just as the balloon is about to take off Toto runs after a cat and Dorothy follows him. Unable to stop, the Wizard leaves without Dorothy. Glinda appears and tells her that she always had the power to return home, but that she needed to learn for herself that she didn't have to run away to find her heart's desire. She bids her friends goodbye, then, following Glinda's instructions, she closes her eyes, taps her heels together three times, and repeats, "There's no place like home."

Dorothy awakens in her bedroom in Kansas, surrounded by family and friends, and tells them of her journey. Although Auntie Em assures her it was all a dream, Dorothy insists it was real and promises never to run away from home again.

Chap. 1 — THE WIZARD OF OZ
Study Guide, Week One, Potential

Principle Scripture

Behold, I am with you and will keep you wherever you go, and will bring you back to this land; for I will not leave you until I have done that of which I have spoken to you. —GENESIS 28:15

The Potential Principle

Running away is not typically the best way to solve a problem, but in *The Wizard of Oz* that's what Dorothy did to save Toto's life. Dorothy must have wondered if running was a good idea when she saw where her house had landed after the cyclone blew her into Oz. As she uttered one of the most famous lines in movie history, "Toto, I've a feeling we're not in Kansas anymore," she probably regretted running and not solving her problem in a different way. Most of us have run away at one time or another, whether from a relationship, a job, finances, or even ourselves. The saddest running we do in our lives is when we run away from God instead of into his loving arms.

Principle Ponderings

1. What could Dorothy have done differently to save Toto and stay home?
2. Who helped her figure out that running away was not the answer?
3. What was Dorothy running toward as she left Oz?

Principle Philosophies

1. You can run, but at some point you will always run out of road.
2. You can't hide from God.
3. Running can weaken you for the eventual battle.

Principle Passages

1. Running away will never make you free.
   —Kenny Loggins
2. We all flee in hope of finding some ground of security
   —M. T. Anderson
3. Sometimes humans beg for battles to be taken away from them, not realizing that only in struggling with shadows is the Light made manifest.
   —W. Michael Gear

Principle Possibilities

1. How are we taught to deal with a problem biblically?
2. Have you ever dodged or run away from a problem even though you knew you were making it worse by not dealing with it right then?
3. Were there long-term ramifications because you ran instead of confronting the problem?

Principle Point ❧

The first actor considered for the title role was W. C. Fields. Because the role as originally written was thought to be too small, additional roles were added in the hope that the longer screen time would woo the actor to accept the role. That's why the actor who accepted the role, Frank Morgan, plays the Wizard, Professor Marvel, the gatekeeper, the guard, and the driver with the "horse with a different color."

Chap. 1 — THE WIZARD OF OZ
Study Guide, Week Two, Potential

Principle Scripture

And he said to man, "Behold, the fear of the Lord, that is wisdom; and to depart from evil is understanding." —Job 28:28

The Potential Principle

After Dorothy brings back the broom to the great and powerful Oz, she and her companions are given an audience to make their requests. The scarecrow has long been plagued with frustrations because he says he doesn't have a brain. In reality what he wants he already has: wisdom. The Wizard confers upon him an honorary degree of Th.D. or, as he explains, Doctor of Thinkology.

Principle Ponderings

1. Was the scarecrow yearning for a physical brain or to be an active, successful part of society?

2. How did the scarecrow show that he was intelligent in the ways that mattered?
3. How did Dorothy, the lion, and the Tin Man show their intelligence during their journey?

Principle Philosophies

1. There are an awful lot of dumb smart people out there.
2. Common sense should be called uncommon sense because it's getting harder and harder to find.
3. Some of the smartest people are those with the lowest IQ.

Principle Passages

1. The true sign of intelligence is not knowledge but imagination. —Albert Einstein
2. Some of the world's greatest feats were accomplished by people not smart enough to know they were impossible.
 —Doug Larson
3. Everybody is a genius. But if you judge a fish by its ability to climb a tree, it will spend it's whole life thinking it's stupid. —Albert Einstein

Principle Possibilities

1. Your true potential is God-given, and that includes your intelligence. Do you appreciate that God made you exactly as God needed you to be?
2. It's better to be wise than it is to be smart. Do you read and study God's word to achieve wisdom?
3. Are you learning from your life experiences so that you know that you should believe only half of what you hear so that you can know which half is the right half?

Principle Point ☙

In the book Dorothy's slippers were silver, and that's how it was set to be in the film, However, MGM head Louis B. Mayer decided that with a Technicolor production the slippers should be changed to ruby colored.

Chap. 1 — THE WIZARD OF OZ
Study Guide, Week Three, Potential

Principle Scripture

Above all, maintain consistant love for one another, for love covers a multitude of sins. —1 PETER 4:8

The Potential Principle

The Tin Man bemoaned his lack of a heart. "As for you, my galvanized friend, you want a heart. You don't know how lucky you are not to have one. Hearts will never be practical until they can be made unbreakable," said the Wizard. "But I still want one," replied the Tin Man. A heart is a muscle that allows the body to keep living. When we talk about heart we mean compassion and love. The Wizard really had no power, and he was wrong about most things, but he was 100 percent right when he said, "A heart is not judged by how much you love, but by how much you are loved by others." After her three friends have received their presentations, the Wizard asks Dorothy what she has learned. "Well, I . . . I think that it . . . it wasn't enough to just want to see Uncle Henry and Auntie Em. . . and it's that. . . if I ever go looking for my heart's desire again, I won't look any furher than my own back yard . . . Because if it isn't there, I never really lost it to begin with! Is that right?"

Principle Ponderings

1. How do we know that the Tin Man had great capacity to love and to be loved?

2. Dorothy's love for Toto is what put her on the road to Oz. Who else did she love and how did she show that love?

3. What other characters showed love along the way and to whom?

Principle Philosophies

1. By treating people the way they ought to be treated, you help them be the person God meant them to be.

2. Sometimes the best way to show love is to criticize, but only if you have a heart to help.

3. What's in a person's heart is between that person and God.

Principle Passages

1. In prayer it is better to have a heart without words than words without a heart. —Mahatma Gandhi

2. While you are proclaiming peace with your lips, be careful to have it even more fully in your heart.
—St. Francis of Assisi

3. Great thoughts and a pure heart: that is what we should ask from God. —Johann Wolfgang Von Goethe

Principle Possibilities

1. Has your capacity to love the unlovable kept pace with your spiritual growth? What is stopping you from loving lavishly?

2. What is one significant thing you did for love expecting nothing in return? How did it make you feel? Was it worth it?

3. What is your personal definition of love? Do you pursue love or does it come naturally? What do you do on a

daily basis to ensure you are showing the love of Christ to family, friends, and strangers?

Principle Point ℘

Buddy Ebsen (Jed Clampett in *The Beverly Hillbillies*), left the production as the Tin Man due to an allergic reaction to silver dust make-up, and Jack Haley replaced him.

Chap. 1 — THE WIZARD OF OZ
Study Guide, Week Four, Potential

Principle Scripture

Have no anxiety about anything, but in everything by prayer and supplication with thanksgiving let your requests be made known to God. And the peace of God, which passes all understanding, will keep your hearts and your minds in Christ Jesus.

—PHILIPPIANS 4:6–7

The Potential Principle

"Courage! What makes a king out of a slave? Courage! What makes the flag on the mast to wave? Courage! What makes the elephant charge his tusk in the misty mist, or the dusky dusk? What makes the muskrat guard his musk? Courage! What makes the sphinx the seventh wonder? Courage! What makes the dawn come up like thunder? Courage! What makes the Hottentot so hot? What puts the 'ape' in apricot? What have they got that I ain't got?" The Cowardly Lion's familiar soliloquy mirrors how many of us think of courage. The Wizard set him on the path to understanding what true courage is. "You, my friend," he explained, "are a victim of disorganized thinking. You are under the unfortunate impression that just because you run away you have no courage; you're confusing courage with wisdom."

Principle Ponderings

1. Do you consider the Cowardly Lion courageous? What is the definition of courage?

2. Was Dorothy courageous or just reactive to situations?

3. Who was the most courageous of the four travelers?

Principle Philosophies

1. It takes more effort than courage to unlock our potential.

2. You can change your future no matter your past if you muster up the courage to do so

3. All the courage we need is in God's word.

Principle Passages

1. Only a person of worth can recognize the worth in others. —THOMAS CARLYLE

2. For the Lord will be your confidence and will keep your foot from being caught. —NAHUM 1:7

3. Be strong and of good courage, do not fear or be in dread of them: for it is the Lord your God who goes with you; he will not fail you or forsake you.
—DEUTERONOMY 31:6

Principle Possibilities

1. What is the most courageous thing you have ever done? Was it for you or someone else?

2. Failure is not final if you have the courage to dig out of your hole. What size shovel do you need to dig out of your hole?

3. Without courage no other virtue matters. Do you make it a daily habit to practice courage?

Principle Point ✐
The horses in the Emerald City palace were colored with Jell-O crystals. Those scenes had to be shot quickly so that the horses didn't lick off the sweet Jell-O.

MORE THAN A BEAUTY QUEEN

It takes courage to grow up
and turn out to be
who you really are.
—e e cummings

In 2001 Julia Roberts won an Oscar for her performance as Erin Brockovich, a personal injury victim turned legal researcher and advocate. The real-life Brockovich used a legal slingshot to fell the goliath Pacific Gas & Electric, but taking into account her looks and life experiences, no one would have dreamed she had the potential to make such a difference in so many lives. The youngest child of an industrial engineer father and a journalist mother, Brockovitch grew up in Lawrence, Kansas. She credits her parents with her future success because they always believed she could do anything she wanted.

Her first job after moving to California was as a management trainee for K-Mart. It was not a good fit for her, and so she decided to begin, but never finished, a degree in electrical engineering. After winning the 1981 Miss Pacific Coast beauty pageant she gave up pageant life, married, moved back to Kansas, and had two children. Eventually she and her family settled in Reno, Nevada. A subsequent divorce followed by two marriages and divorces left Brockovich a single mother with three children and not many options.

Her story could have paralleled that of countless single mothers had it not been for her determination and potential. In Romans 8:28 we learn that "in everything God works for good with those who love him, who are called according to his purpose." Her Romans 8:28 moment might have been the automobile accident that led her to personal injury lawyer Ed Masry. The small settlement awarded did not allow her to be a stay-at-home mother, and she started work as a file clerk for the firm that had represented her.

Brockovich, who suffers from dyslexia, developed a learning style focused on memorization. Many people let a diagnosis of dyslexia define their potential, but it is because of her unique way of doing her job that Brockovitch was able to pay attention to details and look for commonalities in her stack of medical records until a pattern emerged. Her dogged determination led her to believe that Pacific Gas & Electric had been poisoning the small town of Hinkley's water for over thirty years.

In *The Wizard of Oz*, Dorothy already had the potential to make it home; she just didn't know it. Like Dorothy, the former beauty queen from Kansas always had potential; she just had to figure it out.

Thanks to Brockovich's tenacity, in 1996 Pacific Gas & Electric paid out the largest toxic tort injury settlement in U.S. history: $333 million in damages to more than six hundred Hinkley residents who had been exposed to leaking toxic Chromium 6 in their ground water.

One of the best arguments for discovering our potential comes from Audrey Hepburn. "Nothing is impossible; the word itself says 'I'm possible'!" An even better one comes from Matthew 19:26, when Jesus said, "With men this is impossible, but with God all things are possible." God wants us to live our full potential and, with God, all things really are possible.

— TWO —

Principle Scripture
"For I know the plans I have for you," declares the Lord, "plans to prosper you and not to harm you, plans to give you hope and a future. —JEREMIAH 29:11

The Transformative Power of
PURPOSE

Hugo

DREAM BIG!

> *If you can't figure out your purpose,*
> *figure out your passion.*
> *For your passion will lead you*
> *right into your purpose.*
> —BISHOP T. D. JAKES

As soon as we heard the strains of "When You Wish upon a Star" every Sunday evening we would all rush downstairs to watch *The Wonderful World of Disney*. The cartoons and movies, and even Walt Disney as the host, made it one of the defining shows of my childhood, as it was for millions each week.

From an early age Walt Disney had a purpose. He dreamed big dreams, and he made us believe that if we wished upon a star our dreams would come true too. He made what he created look effortless, but the opposite was true.

Despite knowing his purpose in life his road to success was filled with failures and frustrations. He experienced bankruptcy at the age of twenty two. Unintentional copyright infringement leading to the loss of his company and all but one of his artists caused another setback. With the success of *Snow White and the Seven Dwarfs*, Walt Disney and his brother, Roy, built a home for their parents. What should have be a wonderful season of their lives turned tragic with the death of his mother from carbon monoxide poisoning in the poorly constructed house. Despite these and many other challenges Walt Disney went on to create an empire that has continued to delight millions of families every day.

In the movie *Hugo* pioneer filmmaker George Mèliès, like Walt Disney, had both successes and failures in the movie industry. A magical journey set in Paris in 1931, *Hugo* brilliantly weaves the humble beginnings of silent film into a story about the quest for purpose as seen through the eyes Hugo Cabret, a young boy searching for his purpose in life.

Walt Disney reminded us that "we keep moving forward, opening new doors, and doing new things, because we're curious and curiosity keeps leading us down new paths." That is exactly what Hugo and his newfound friend, Isabelle, did as their search for a key led them to help someone rediscover their purpose and their passion.

> *One of the most legendary directors of our time takes us on an extraordinary adventure.*

pur•pose. *noun.* The object toward which one strives or for which something exists; an aim or a goal

Living a full life begins with having a purpose. German-born theologian Albert Schweitzer said, "The purpose of human life is to serve, and to show compassion and the will to help others." In this chapter we explore the importance of understanding God's purpose for our life and doing everything possible to fulfil that purpose.

Synopsis

Sometimes it's children who lead adults to rediscover what they once knew, and that's how it is in the visually stunning Academy

HUGO 33

Award winning movie *Hugo*. Filled with a childlike sense of wonder, adventure, comedy, beautiful images, and a moving score, *Hugo* is first and foremost a story about finding one's purpose and gifts in life.

Hugo Cabret (Asa Butterfield) is a recently orphaned boy secretly living in the Paris train station in 1931. His alcoholic uncle, the station clock master, becomes his guardian after his beloved father's death. Hugo is forced to quit school and begin running the elaborate clocks. His uncle suddenly disappears and Hugo continues living in the recesses of the Paris train station stealing food from the vendors to survive as he continues tending the clocks. But Hugo has a secret.

After becoming an orphan, Hugo is left with his inherited mechanical ability and the abandoned, broken automaton robot they worked on together before his father's death. Hugo is confident he can fix the robot if he can find enough pieces. With no money, he steals from an old man named Georges (Ben Kingsley), who runs a watch and toy repair shop in the train station. When Hugo is caught trying to steal a mechanical toy mouse, Georges takes away Hugo's journal of notes his father kept related to the mechanical man and threatens to burn it at his home. Hugo follows him home and meets Georges's goddaughter and fellow orphan, Isabelle (Chloe Grace Moretz).

He explains to Isabelle the importance of the journal and that he was stealing the parts from Georges to fix up the mechanical man. Georges leads Hugo to believe he destroyed Hugo's beloved journal, but Isabelle reveals that her godfather didn't really burn it. Hugo confronts Georges and, as a way of paying for the stolen items, Hugo begins to work in the shop hoping that he will get his journal returned.

One day Hugo discovers that Isabelle is wearing a heart-shaped pendant that might be the missing key required to wind up the mechanical man. At first they are disappointed when the robot writes only what appears to be random marks and stops. Soon, however, the robot starts up a second time, but instead of writing words, the robot draws a picture of the man in the moon with a small rocket in its eye. Hugo remembers the image from having heard his father describe it as part of the first movie he had ever seen. When the robot signs the name Georges Méliès at the bottom, Isabelle reveals that her godfather Georges's last name is Méliès.

Hugo and Isabelle show the picture to her godmother, who cautions them not to show Georges because he has tried to put his painful past behind him. Hugo and Isabelle go on a quest to unravel the mysterious story. They learn that Georges Méliès, a former filmmaker—and real true-life figure—made hundreds of movies and helped pioneer the industry before World War I destroyed his career, leaving him bitter and depressed.

After learning this truth about her godfather, Hugo and Isabelle develop a plan to help Georges re-live the significance of his work and remember the legacy he created. With the help of a film historian Hugo and Isabelle ultimately show her godparent's Georges's last surviving film. Thanks to a boy searching for his purpose a man is finally able to embrace life and discover the possibilities.

Hugo, based on the 2007 Brian Selznick novel *The Invention of Hugo Cabret,* is an enchanting film focused on helping us understand that to be the person we are meant to be we must first find our purpose.

Chap. 2 — HUGO
Study Guide, Week One, Purpose

Principle Scripture
But our commonwealth is in heaven, and from it we await a Savior, the Lord Jesus Christ. —Philippians 3:20

The Purpose Principle
The last voice we hear at the end of the movie is that of Isabelle as she begins to write Hugo's story in her journal. "Once

HUGO

upon a time, I met a boy named Hugo Cabret. He lived in a train station. Why did he live in a train station? you might well ask. That's really what this book is going to be about. And about how this singular young man searched so hard to find a secret message from his father, and how that message led his way, all the way home." Hugo's quest to find his purpose, and to hear a message from his father, parallel's our own search for meaning in our lives. We yearn to hear God's message, a call to come home.

Principle Ponderings

1. During most of the movie Hugo looks forlorn. Why is that?
2. How did Hugo become an orphan and how did losing his father change his life?
3. Hugo has no physical home in the traditional sense and no one to love him or accept his love. What kept him going?

Principle Philosophies

1. They say love makes a house a home. Purpose is right up there as well.
2. Home is where our journey begins and ends.
3. Reaching your true home is an adventure in faith.

Principle Passages

1. The ache for home lives in all of us, the safe place where we can go as we are and not be questioned.
   —MAYA ANGELOU
2. God is at home; it's we who have gone out for a walk.
   —MEISTER ECKHART
3. My home is in heaven. I'm just traveling through this world. —BILLY GRAHAM

Principle Possibilities

1. When Hugo meets Isabelle, he asks if she would like to have an adventure. Most adventures start with a story. How and why are stories essential to the human experience?
2. Do you still have adventures? If not, why? How can you recapture the childlike delight inspired by stories and adventures?
3. Do you daily hear God's promise that no matter how difficult life can be, there is a home for you?

Principle Point ❧

Director Martin Scorsese's young daughter, Francesca, gave her father a copy of Brian Selznick's book *The Invention of Hugo Cabret* as a birthday gift, hoping he would make it into a film one day.

Chap. 2 — HUGO
Study Guide, Week Two, Purpose

Principle Scripture

Hope deferred makes the heart sick, but a desire fulfilled is a tree of life. —Proverbs 13:12

The Purpose Principle

As believers what is our true purpose? At one point Hugo and Isabelle are in the train station looking down on the lights of Paris. Hugo explains his theory to Isabelle. "I'd imagine the whole world was one big machine. Machines never come with any extra parts, you know. They always come with the exact amount they need. So I figured, if the entire world was one big machine, I couldn't be an extra part. I had to be here for some reason. And that means you have to be here for some reason, too."

If we believe as Hugo does, that each person on this earth has a purpose, how are we to find it?

Principle Ponderings

1. When the movie begins, what is Hugo's purpose? How did his purpose change? Did the new purpose align with the old one?
2. How do his relationships with Georges and Isabelle help him to find and later redefine his purpose?
3. Through helping others we also help ourselves. Is that the case with Hugo and Isabelle?

Principle Philosophies

1. Our purpose is to find and pursue our purpose.
2. Anyone can find a purpose. Finding God's purpose is infinitely more difficult and more rewarding.
3. God has a bigger plan than you do for the rest of your life.

Principle Passages

1. Accept yourself, your strengths, your weaknesses, your truths, and know what tools you have to fulfill your purpose. —Steve Maraboli
2. God created us for this: to live our lives in a way that makes him look more like the greatness and the beauty and the infinite worth that he really is. This is what it means to be created in the image of God. —John Piper
3. God can make you anything you want to be, but you have to put everything in His hands.
   —Mahalia Jackson

Principle Possibilities

1. Do you believe that we can reach our full potential only if we have a living, breathing relationship with God? Why or why not?

2. Beyond our spiritual purpose on earth, does everybody have a specific destiny to fulfil? What is your destiny?

3. Hugo eventually found someone to believe in his purpose, someone who saw it as an adventure. Have you been blessed with people to support you in reaching your potential? If not, how have you continued? Or have you?

Principle Point 〜

Hugo was Martin Scorsese's first PG rated film in eighteen years.

Chap. 2 — HUGO
Study Guide, Week Three, Purpose

Principle Scripture

And hope does not disappoint us, because God's love has been poured into our hearts through the Holy Spirit, which has been given to us. —Romans 5:5

The Purpose Principle

Hugo loves machines. His first purpose is to get the broken automaton robot to work. At one point he explains to Isabelle the grief he feels over broken machines. "Maybe that's why a broken machine always makes me a little sad, because it isn't able to do what it was meant to do . . . Maybe it's the same with people. If you lose your purpose, it's like you're broken." His quest to fix the broken machine leads him on the road to fixing damaged lives, including his own.

Principle Ponderings

1. From where did Hugo's brokenness come? Who else thought that their life was shattered beyond fixing?

2. On the surface the station inspector is a secondary character. He was injured in the war and is convinced that he will never heal. Is he talking only about his leg? Does his

struggle and subsequent growth mirror the film's major plotline?

3. The war impacted Georges's dreams and his life. How did his bitterness change him and those around him?

Principle Philosophies

1. Things that matter are irreparably broken only if you think they are.
2. No matter how shattered your life, an intact faith is the answer.
3. God is in the fix it business.

Principle Passages

1. The Christian life is not a constant high. I have my moments of deep discouragement. I have to go to God in prayer with tears in my eyes, and say, "O God, forgive me," or "Help me." —Billy Graham
2. Your talent is God's gift to you. What you do with it is your gift back to God. —Leo Buscaglia
3. It is not death that a man should fear, but he should fear never beginning to live. —Marcus Aurelius

Principle Possibilities

1. Was there ever a time when you thought you or a dream was broken beyond repair? How did you continue on? Are you still doing self-repair with or without God's help?
2. Do you believe that God can heal any brokenness in your life?
3. Do you look for opportunities to help others move from hopeless to hope?

Principle Point ˜
Hugo was Martin Scorsese's first feature film in twelve years not starring Leonardo DiCaprio.

Chap. 2 — HUGO
Study Guide, Week Four, Purpose

Principle Scripture
But you are a chosen race, a royal priesthood, a holy nation, God's own people, that you may declare the wonderful deeds of him who called you out of darkness into his marvelous light.

—1 Peter 2:9

The Purpose Principle
Before he has a renewed sense of joy Georges says, "My life has taught me one lesson, Hugo Cabret, and not the one I thought it would. Happy endings only happen in the movies." Of course after Hugo and Isabelle discover Georges's history and learn about his illustrious career, everything changes. By the end of the movie Georges, and others who have displayed brokenness, including Hugo himself, discover that there is such a thing as a happy ending.

Principle Ponderings
1. Why was Georges so resistant to hope?
2. Who else did not believe in happy endings? Did their opinions change by the end of the movie?
3. How did Hugo change throughout the course of the movie?

Principle Philosophies
1. There will be no end to happy endings for those who trust and obey God's word.

HUGO

2. You can change the ending to your own story. It's up to you.
3. You can have unhappy chapters in your life book and still have a happy ending.

Principle Passages

1. Great things are not done by impulse, but by a series of small things brought together. —VINCENT VAN GOGH
2. Make your work to be in keeping with your purpose. —LEONARDO DA VINCI
3. Here is a test to find out whether your mission in life is complete. If you're alive, it isn't. —LAUREN BACALL

Principle Possibilities

1. Actress Gilda Radner said, "I wanted a perfect ending. Now I've learned, the hard way, that some poems don't rhyme, and some stories don't have a clear beginning, middle, and end." What do you think she meant by this and how can we apply that to our lives?
2. Does having a happy ending mean there is never unhappiness?
3. Do you believe that fulfilling God's purpose is a way to a happy ending?

Principle Point ↝

Actor Ben Kingsley used director Martin Scorsese as the basis for his character Geroges Mèliès.

WE LOVE LUCY

> *True happiness ... is not attained through self-gratification, but through fidelity to a worthy purpose.*
> —HELEN KELLER

She wasn't a natural redhead, but she was a genius at making us laugh. From an early age Lucille Ball had one purpose; to entertain. As is often the case with funny people, Lucille's early years were anything but filled with humor. Lucille once shared, probably reflecting on her own childhood, "Comedians don't laugh. I don't know why. Perhaps they were sad children."

Despite, or perhaps because of, her sad childhood, she was determined to follow her purpose: Lucille was the daughter of a telephone lineman who died when she was four. When her mother remarried, she was sent to live with her stepfather's parents in upstate New York while her brother, Fred, stayed with their real grandparents. In several interviews she told how her grim step grandmother put a dog collar on her and leashed her to an overhead wire in the backyard so they knew where she was at all times.

Lonely and sad, Lucille invented Sassafrassa, an imaginary friend who assured her that she would be a movie star when she grew up. Lucille found a willing audience at school recess. She brought clothes and hats from home and delighted her classmates with jokes, songs, and dances.

Her first professional step in fulfilling her purpose came not in acting but as a fifteen-year-old model. When she was seventeen Lucille was paralyzed below the hips after a bout with rheumatic fever. She spent three years in a wheelchair refusing to believe she would never walk again. One night she decided to try on her own and took five steps. She did fall flat on her face, but through stubborn determination she eventually walked.

She finally landed a bit part in a movie when she was twenty-two. Wanting to stand out, she dyed her hair bright red, and the Lucy we have known and loved for generations began to emerge. The roles continued, rarely the star, and at thirty-nine, to salvage both her marriage to Desi Arnaz and her career, they decided to do a television sitcom together.

Her road to success wasn't easy, but she pursued her purpose with determination to become the first lady of television. Lucille became a multimillionaire with Desilu Studio, the world's largest production facility. After buying out Desi for $2.5 million, she eventually sold the corporation to Gulf and Western for $17 million.

It wasn't the money, however, that the Lucy we love counted as success. When asked her definition of a successful woman she answered, "A successful woman is one with a great desire, an overwhelming motive, all the time, year after year, to make people happy."

I Love Lucy ran from 1951 to 1957 but over sixty years after the first episode aired, the sitcom has dominated the worldwide syndication market. Whether it's the Viteameatavegamin episode, the one where she stomped grapes, worked on the candy line, or mimed with Harpo Marx, Lucille Ball's purpose never changed. She wanted to make us laugh. That's why we love Lucy.

—THREE—

Principle Scripture
Trust in the Lord with all your heart and lean not on your own understanding; in all your ways acknowledge him, and he will make your paths straight. —PROVERBS 3:5–6

The Transformative Power of
PRIORITIES

Mr. Holland's Opus

IT'S A WONDERFUL LIFE

> *Good things happen when you get your priorities straight.*
> —SCOTT CAAN

Mr. Smith Goes to Washington, *Vertigo*, *Rear Window*, and *Harvey*. Can you imagine anyone other than Jimmy Stewart starring in these and other great classics? Had Stewart pursued his first dream he would not have been an actor, much less a star.

Jimmy Stewart's priority in life was to be an architect. In fact, while an undergraduate at Princeton, he wrote such an impressive thesis on airport design that he was offered a full graduate scholarship. We might be flying out of Stewart-designed airports instead of enjoying his films had he not graduated during the Great Depression.

When asked how he became an actor Stewart answered, "Nobody was putting up any buildings at the time. Yet the theater was exploding." In one of those serendipitous twists he decided that because he had enjoyed acting in college, he might as well try to earn a living in the theater. He moved to New York, appeared in several plays, and, despite no formal training, was asked to do some Hollywood screen tests where studio heads believed in him and gave him a chance.

Jimmy Stewart had one purpose for his life, but thankfully God had another. He became famous not for skyscrapers or housing developments, but for his collaborations with directors such as Frank Capra and Alfred Hitchcock.

Like Jimmy Stewart, in *Mr. Holland's Opus,* Gene Holland, a passionate musician who dreams of composing one truly memorable piece of music, discovers his life's work after realizing that his priority of becoming rich and famous was not God's priority. After reluctantly accepting a "day job" as a high school music teacher to support his family, Mr. Holland keeps his priorities straight over a thirty-year span and sees the impact he's had on the world around him. Because they had their priorities straight, by the end of Jimmy Stewart's days and the closing scene of *Mr. Holland's Opus,* both men could truly say, "It's been a wonderful life."

*Life is what happens to you
while you're busy making other plans.*

pri•or•i•ties. *noun.* **Something important that must be done first or needs more attention than anything else**

Once we have determined our purpose, only by setting priorities can we finish the race. American clergyman Russell M. Nelson was right when he said, "Your life will be a blessed and balanced experience if you first honor your identity and priority." Chapter 3 focuses on how we as busy people must make and stand by priorities based on God's commandments.

Synopsis

Thirty-year-old Glenn Holland (Richard Dreyfuss) is a musician with his priorities in place. As is the case for many, if not most, artists, his music doesn't pay the bills, and he decides to take a job teaching at John F. Kennedy High School. This sabbatical from full-time music will allow him to save enough money to quit in a few years and write music. Besides, he can compose after school and weekends, and he will have summer breaks. His supportive wife, Iris (Glenne Headly), reminds him that it's just a gig and so the story unfolds.

Mr. Holland's less than stellar start with Vice-Principal Wolters (William H. Macy) and Principal Jacobs (Olivia Dukakis) leaves him flustered and rethinking his decision. Within minutes of entering his first class he realizes that the students are universally apathetic and mostly terrible musicians. His day is somewhat salvaged when he meets football coach Bill Meister (Jay Thomas) and begins a lifelong friendship, but he is still ready to quit. Iris reminds him that if everything goes as they have carefully planned, he should be able to quit in four years and pursue his dreams.

Mr. Holland soon learns that teaching high school music is much more than a gig. Principle Jacobs explains to him that "a teacher has two jobs: fill young minds with knowledge, yes, but more important, give those minds a compass so that that knowledge doesn't go to waste." It doesn't happen overnight, but at first by accident and eventually by design his priorities shift from writing his opus to making a difference in the lives of his students.

Grading papers, starting a marching band, helping students before and after school, and summer driver's education somehow steal all that "extra" time. The amount of time he is able to devote to his passion shrinks as his school duties expand and he despairs of ever completing his opus.

In his first burst of creativity Glenn decides to try some unconventional methods of teaching music appreciation. He demonstrates to the students the similarities between Bach's *Minuet in G* and rock-and-roll in the form of the Toys' *Lover's Concerto*. The new teaching approach is a success, and Mr. Holland returns home excited for the first time since becoming a teacher. Mr. Holland reaches out to a number of students and grows from babysitting bored teenagers to becoming everyone's favorite teacher.

Mr. Holland continually has to shift his priorities as he learns Iris is pregnant, uses their savings, takes on extra work to buy a home, and learns that his son, Cole, is deaf. Cole's deafness is a crushing disappointment to his father, who had hopes of sharing his passion for music with his son. After many struggles Glenn discovers Cole listening to records by sitting on the speakers and feeling the vibrations through his body. They draw closer thanks to their shared love of music.

At one point Glenn becomes interested in a talented young singer named Rowena Morgan, who has the starring role in the school musical revue. After the revue, Rowena tells Mr. Holland that she will be leaving for New York after the last performance and that she'd like him to come with her. He is tempted to leave everything behind and go with Rowena; however, he realizes how much he loves Iris and decides to focus on his ever changing priorities.

As with too many schools in America, Principal Wolters announces that, due to budget cuts, Art, Music, and Drama have been cut from the school curriculum. "It's almost funny," Mr. Holland, tells his old nemesis when he learns he will be out of a job, "I got dragged into this gig kicking and screaming, and now it's the only thing I want to do."

On his final day, Iris and Cole lead him to the auditorium, where a surprise going-away celebration is taking place. The emcee, the red haired clarinettist he first encouraged, has since become the state's governor. Governor Lang ends her heartwarming speech by telling Mr. Holland how much he is appreciated. "There is not a life in this room that you have not touched, and each of us is a better person because of you. We are your symphony Mr. Holland. We are the melodies and the notes of your opus. We are the music of your life."

Mr. Holland's Opus stresses love of family, self-sacrifice, and marital fidelity. It also reminds us that when we have our priorities in order, believing in people can have an impact in the lives of many over a lifetime.

Chap. 3 — MR. HOLLAND'S OPUS
Study Guide, Week One, Priorities

Principle Scripture
Commit your work to the Lord, and your plans will be established. —Proverbs 16:3

The Priority Principle
Mr. Holland knows exactly what he wants to achieve in life, and nothing is going to stop him. He has talent, a beautiful wife, and a plan, and that's enough to succeed. The tagline of the movie says, "Life is what happens to you while you're busy making other plans," and that is exactly what happens to Glenn Holland. Getting your priorities straight can help you use your gifts and live a full and compelling life. Learning to reorder those priorities into God's priorities is of even greater importance.

Principle Ponderings
1. What is Mr. Holland's plan in the beginning of the movie? How does teaching play a role in his plan?
2. Do you agree or disagree with the principal when she criticizes Mr. Holland for his attitude toward teaching?
3. What do you think is God's plan for Mr. Holland?

Principle Philosophies
1. Knowing and keeping God's priorities is needed to stay on God's path.
2. Getting your priorities straight is a form of worshiping God.
3. Priorities change; the commandment to love others never does.

Principle Passages

1. And God will meet all your needs according to his glorious riches in Christ Jesus. —Philippians 4:19
2. What we have done for ourselves alone dies with us; what we have done for others and the world remains and is immortal. —Albert Pike
3. It's easy to make a buck. It's a lot tougher to make a difference. —Tom Brokaw

Principle Possibilities

1. Do you and God have the same priorities for your life? If so when and how did it happen?
2. Who believed in you in such a significant way that they made a profound difference in your life? Have you made believing in others a priority at home, at work, at church, and in your community?
3. When you had a plan and it didn't work out, did something better eventually happen?

Principle Point ℘
Every person portrayed as hearing-impaired in the film is also hearing-impaired in real life.

Chap. 3 — MR. HOLLAND'S OPUS
Study Guide, Week Two, Priorities

Principle Scripture
Never flag in zeal, be aglow with the Spirit, serve the Lord.
—Romans 12:11

The Priority Principle
At one point Mr. Holland explains that there is more to music than proficiency. "Playing music is supposed to be fun," he stresses. "It's about heart, it's about feelings, moving people, and something beautiful, and it's not about notes on a page. I can teach you notes on a page, I can't teach you that other stuff."

Mr. Holland first has a passion for music and, eventually, for his students. Having passion about our gifts is a wonderful thing. Having passion about showing God's love to the people in our lives is even better.

Principle Ponderings

1. Acts 20:35 teaches us that it is more blessed to give than to receive. In the beginning was Mr. Holland doing his job in an Acts 20:35 way? Did that ever change? How?

2. What does Mr. Holland say when Vice Principal Wolters and Principal Jacobs call him on using rock 'n' roll to get the students passionate about music?

3. At one point Iris tells her husband that he cares more about his students than he does about his own son? Is that true? What unique way does he find to share his passion with his own son?

Principle Philosophies

1. Renew your passions and your priorities every day.

2. God wants you to use your passions to reach others.

3. Purpose is a starting point, but passion is what will drive you to the finish line.

Principle Passages

1. You can succeed at almost anything for which you have unlimited enthusiasm. —CHARLES M. SCHWAB

2. Nothing great in the world has been accomplished without passion. —GEORGE WILHELM FRIEDRICH HEGEL

3. One person with passion is better than forty people merely interested. —E. M. FORSTER

Principle Possibilities

1. As a Christian is it more important to be defined by what you do or by how you do it?
2. Are you willing to use creative ways to share your passion for the gospel with others?
3. How can you regain your passion once it is lost?

Principle Point ❧

Richard Dreyfuss plays Glenn Holland in the movie. Glenne Headly plays his wife, Iris.

Chap. 3 — MR. HOLLAND'S OPUS
Study Guide, Week Three, Priorities

Principle Scripture

And let us not grow weary in well doing, for in due season we shall reap, if we do not lose heart. —GALATIANS 6:9

The Priority Principle

Early in the film Mr. Holland becomes discouraged because he is torn in two different directions. The origin of the idiom "stuck between a rock and a hard place" is from *The Odyssey*. In ancient Greek mythology, Odysseus must pass between Scylla, a man-eating monster that strikes from the cliffs (the "rock") and Charybdis, a treacherous whirlpool (the "hard place"). Mr. Holland's dilemma might not be as life-threatening as Odysseus, but it was sucking the joy out of his life. Unlike Odysseus, we can always go to God for direction.

Principle Ponderings

1. What scenes in the movie show Mr. Holland being caught between a rock and a hard place?
2. How did he show his discouragement in those scenes?

3. What does he learn about himself, teaching, his students, and his family in the process?

Principle Philosophies

   1. Sometimes not making a choice is making a choice.
   2. The antidote to discouragement is faith.
   3. Seeds of discouragement will not grow in a thankful heart.

Principle Passages

   1. Men, like nails, lose their usefulness when they lose direction and begin to bend. —Walter Savage Landor
   2. Let no feeling of discouragement prey upon you, and in the end you are sure to succeed. —Abraham Lincoln
   3. Disappointments will come and go, but discouragement is a choice that you make. —Dr. Charles Stanley

Principle Possibilities

   1. Have you ever been between a rock and a hard space? What did you learn by the choice you made? How were others affected?
   2. Psalm 32:8 says, "I will instruct you and teach you in the way you should go; I will counsel you with my loving eye on you." How does Psalm 32:8 apply to your own personal choices you make to stay on the right path?
   3. How do we prioritize all the demands on our time, talent, and resources? How do we know when we are giving away too much of ourselves so there's nothing left?

Principle Point ℘

Michael Kaman composed the score for *Mr. Holland's Opus*. He was so inspired by the story that he started Mr. Holland's Opus

Foundation, a non-profit that keeps music alive by donating musical instruments to under-funded music programs.

Chap. 3 — MR. HOLLAND'S OPUS
Study Guide, Week Four, Priorities

Principle Scripture

For the whole law is fulfilled in one word, "You shall love your neighbor as yourself." —GALATIANS 5:14

The Priority Principle

Principle Jacobs tells Mr. Holland that "a teacher has two jobs; fill young minds with knowledge, yes, but more important, give those minds a compass so that that knowledge doesn't go to waste." One of his "compass opportunities" is Gertrude Lang, an aspiring clarinettist. Despite her desire to excel and the extra time he devotes to her before school, she fails miserably. In a burst of inspiration he helps her to understand that she knows the notes in her head and now needs to play them from her heart. That relationship proves to be the turning point, and they both follow their own compass. The relationships are the heart of *Mr. Holland's Opus*. They teach us that, above all, God asks us to love our neighbors as ourselves.

Principle Ponderings

1. Mr. Holland is kind to a number of different students going beyond his job description and making a difference. Who were they and which one touched you the most?

2. In his discouragement Mr. Holland could have escaped his priorities by leaving town with Rowena. Why do you think he stayed with his wife?

3. While Mr. Holland is helping his students, who is helping him become a superb teacher and a man of great character?

Principle Philosophies

1. Rather than criticizing others and making them feel unwanted, we should pick them up and make them feel good.
2. The smallest decisions can change your life forever.
3. Be that person who brings out the best in others.

Principle Passages

1. There is no more lovely, friendly, and charming relationship, communion, or company than a good marriage.
   —Martin Luther
2. Never let a problem to be solved become more important than the person to be loved. —Barbara Johnson
3. Each relationship nurtures a strength or weakness within you. —Mike Murdock

Principle Possibilities

1. It's not natural to care more for others than for one's self. How can we begin to be more Christlike in our actions and reactions toward others?
2. How do the relationships in your life nurture or destroy you? How can you eliminate the latter?
3. Who is your Opus?

Principle Point ꙮ

Just before Mr. Holland conducts his Opus he signs to Cole, "I love you."

THE COMEBACK KID

> *Action expresses priorities.*
> —Mahatma Gandhi

Setting priorities is not always a good thing if the path we are on is the wrong one. Robert Downey Jr. seemed content with the priority he had set for himself, even though those around him knew he was headed in the wrong direction.

Downey's road to drug addiction started at a young age. His father, actor, writer, and director Robert Downey Sr., an admitted drug addict, bonded with his son over marijuana at the age of six. In interviews Downey explained that drug use became an emotional bond between him and his father: "When my dad and I would do drugs together, it was like him trying to express his love for me in the only way he knew how." The drug use increased until Downey's priorities revolved around his drug and alcohol use.

Downey made his acting debut at the age of five, and, despite his escalating drug use, he had an impressive filmography to his credit by the age of thirty. In April 1996, Downey was arrested for possession of heroin, cocaine, and an unloaded handgun while speeding down Sunset Boulevard. In 1999 more arrests and subsequent probation, jail time, and missed court-ordered drug tests led to a three-year prison term at the California Substance Abuse Treatment Facility and State Prison. After nearly a year in prison the judge ruled that his collective time of incarceration since 1996 qualified him for early release.

A week after his release Downey joined the cast of *Ally McBeal* in a role that garnered him a Golden Globe in the Outstanding Supporting Actor in a Comedy Series. Sadly, Downey's priorities seemed slanted more to partying and drugs than to hard work, and before the end of his first season on *Ally McBeal*, Downey was arrested under the influence of a controlled substance and in possession of cocaine and Valium. After his 2001 arrest, producer David E. Kelly fired him from *Ally McBeal*.

Despite the award-winning actor's talent he was considered unemployable. And then it happened. After five years of substance abuse, arrests, rehab, and relapse, Downey, who had lost his wife and career, changed his priorities and went into rehab to get clean and sober.

After his stint in rehab producers were reluctant to hire Downy because of his past history. In the production phase of a movie the producers must put up an insurance bond in case illness, death, or some other situation arises and the movie actor can't complete the project. In Downey's case the insurance underwriters didn't like the odds and his career would have been over had it not been for his friend and fellow actor, Mel Gibson, who believed in Downey's talent and his rehabilitation possibilities.

Gibson, who had co-starred with Downey in the 1990 movie *Air America*, offered to put up Downey's insurance bond, enabling him to get the lead role in the 2003 movie *The Singing Detective*. Since that life-defining moment of generosity on Gibson's part, Downey has become one of the highest grossing movie stars of the past ten years.

Downey credits his wife, Susan, whom he met in 2003 on the set of *Gothika*, with helping him kick his drug and alcohol habits. "There's no understanding for me of the bigger picture in real time in a hands-on way without her," says Downey of the woman he married in 2005. "Because it was the perfect, perfect, perfect matching of personalities and gifts."

Because of his shift in priorities, since 2008 nine movies including *The Ironman, The Avengers,* and *Sherlock Holmes* franchises, have grossed more than $1.5 billion in the U.S. alone, and his name on the marquee is a box-office guarantee. Because of his shift in priorities Downey really is the Comeback Kid.

—FOUR—

Principle Scripture
And why are you anxious about clothing? Consider the lilies of the field, how they grow; they neither toil nor spin; yet I tell you, even Solomon in all his glory was not arrayed like one of these.
—Matthew 6:28–29

The Transformative Power of
PRAYER

Lilies of the Field

MOUNTAIN-MOVING FAITH

Faith does not believe that God can.
It knows that God will.
—Ben Stein

I once heard a story of a small congregation that had built a new sanctuary on a piece of land willed to them by a church member. Ten days before their first service, the local building inspector advised them that an ordinance required more parking spaces for the larger building. Until the parking lot was doubled in size, the new sanctuary could not be used. It wasn't only a matter of money, which would have been bad enough since the church members had used all their resources on the new building, but the only land left was the mountain against which the church had been built.

"We'll just have to move the mountain," explained the pastor the next Sunday morning. Undaunted by the congregation's scepticism, he announced that he would meet that evening with any members who had "mountain-moving faith." All they had to do was to pray for God to move the mountain from their backyard and provide them with enough money to have the land paved and painted before the scheduled dedication service—in exactly one week.

That night fewer than 10 percent of the three hundred members gathered for a congregational prayer session. They didn't blame anyone for the devastating news, nor bicker about how to make the impossible happen. Instead, they prayed for three hours to a God bigger than any problem they could ever face. "We'll open next Sunday as scheduled," the pastor said after the last "amen."

The next morning, a rough-looking construction foreman came, hardhat in hand, to the pastor's study asking a favor. "We're building a new shopping mall in the next county over," he explained. "We need some landfill, and that mountain behind the church is perfect. If you'd be willing to sell us a piece, and if we can have it right away, we'll pay you for the dirt and pave the level area free of charge."

In *Lilies of the Field* Mother Superior has a prayer life to rival the pastor of the small church with mountain-moving faith. They both believe that nothing is impossible with God and that, as Mason Cooley says, "Faith moves mountains, but you have to keep pushing while you are praying." Mother Superior and Homer pushed while she and the nuns prayed.

We know that God always answers prayers but what's exciting is how the difficulties, combined with prayer, tend to make us better followers of Christ. *Lilies of the Field* helps us explore the ways God answers when we call and why it's so important to believe in the power of prayer.

> *Perhaps the most extraordinary story of courage, conflict, and devotion ever filmed!*

prayer. *noun.* **A devout petition to God**

Beware in your prayers, said Andrew Murray, above everything else, of limiting God, not only by unbelief, but also by fancying that you know what he can do. Expect unexpected things above all that we ask or think. We know that God always answers prayers, but what's exciting is how the difficulties combined with prayers tend to make us better followers of Christ. This chapter explores the ways God answers prayer and why it's so important to pray unceasingly.

Synopsis

In 1963 Sidney Poitier won an Academy Award for his portrayal of Homer Smith, a traveling handyman/jack-of-all-trades who lives on the road in his station wagon. When *Lilies of the Field* begins, Homer stops at a convent in the Arizona desert to replenish his water supply. He finds himself in the midst of a group of German-speaking nuns who have escaped from the Communist-held portion of Berlin and settled in this remote desert community. Despite the language barrier the nuns are attempting to serve the largely Hispanic community.

After Mother Superior, played by Austrian-born Lilia Skala, persuades Homer to do a small roofing repair he stays overnight believing that he will be paid in the morning. Unbeknownst to Homer, the nuns have no money, subsisting on what vegetables the arid climate provides and some milk and eggs. Despite his better judgment, after being stonewalled for payment, Homer agrees to stay another day to help the nuns with other small jobs.

The only house of worship in the area is a mobile field chapel serviced by an itinerant priest who travels to the many small towns in the area providing masses, weddings, christenings, and funerals. Before Homer's arrival Mother Maria determines that, despite their impoverished state, God wanted them to build a chapel. After observing Homer's strength, construction skills, and tools, Mother Maria is convinced that "Schmitt" has been sent from above to help her realize her dream of a "shapel."

While Homer Smith plays the pivotal role, to my way of thinking it is Mother Maria who made the biggest difference. She prays that God will supply everything needed to build the chapel, including, as it turns out, a contractor in the person of Homer Smith.

Before Homer arrives on the scene, Mother Maria manages to get some bricks donated for her cause. Soon after Homer began working on the chapel the bricks are gone and she promises more, even when there is no visible means of getting them. Mother Superior prays about the bricks, but she also writes letters asking for donations; and as she writes, she continues praying. But her prayers are answered in a different way than she ever imagined.

"I failed because I put my faith in people instead of in God," insists the disheartened nun when midway through the movie Homer runs out of bricks. Mother Maria was on the right track when she prayed, but God had something more important to teach her and those whose lives she was destined to influence.

When her appeal for more bricks goes unanswered Mother Maria thinks she can't trust people any longer. There is no way that the poor village people can come up with enough bricks to complete the chapel, but God knew they could play an important role in his creative answer to Mother Maria's prayers.

During his time in the little desert community Homer, who lived on his own and trusted only himself, learns that he doesn't have a market on all the good ideas. He also learns to rely on others, but it isn't easy or without conflict.

Homer has the tools and draws up his plans to accomplish Mother Maria's goal, but his unwillingness to listen to others and work with a team almost derails the project. Instead, he wants to build it on his own despite knowing nothing about working with adobe.

Homer Smith's helpers use their feet to mix affordable and available materials that have been used for generations. The resulting bricks are more suited to the arid desert than traditional building material.

God not only answers Mother Maria's prayer for a chapel, but also strengthens the faith of all involved, which is infinitely more important than a building. Even the village priest who has been holding church services outdoors in the back of a pie wagon, is affected by the manner in which God answered Mother Maria's prayers.

Mother Superior never does get enough bricks to complete her chapel, but it is finished despite the shortfall. Because of the way God answers her prayers, Mother Maria gets not just a chapel but a renewed faith in people and their ability and willingness to help reach a goal.

Lilies of the Field is full of lessons about prayer and humility, and the last scene teaches us the most valuable lesson of all.

"It's all finished. I done builded you a chapel," Homer says to Mother Superior after completing the finishing touches. Homer then gathers the nuns for what will be their final English lesson.

"I build a chapel," he says.

The smiling nuns repeat in lyrical, accented English, "I build a chapel."

Pointing a finger at the nuns, Homer moves on to the next pronoun. "You build a chapel."

Again the nuns parrot his phrase, "You build a chapel."

Throughout the movie Homer learns that building a chapel was a group effort and he proudly proclaims with a sweep of his hands, "We build a chapel."

"No," Mother Superior interrupts before the sisters pipe in. Pointing toward heaven, she says, "He build a chapel."

In *Lilies of the Field* we know from the start that the chapel will be completed; we just don't know all the steps involved. When we believe in ourselves it's the same; we don't know all the steps we will need to reach the goal, but we can be assured that through prayer God will be with us every step of the way.

Chap. 4 — LILIES OF THE FIELD
Study Guide, Week One, Prayer

Principle Scripture
And I tell you, you are Peter, and on this rock I will build my church, and the powers of death shall not prevail against it.

—Matthew 16:18

The Prayer Principle
Prayer is simply talking to God, how we communicate our thoughts, needs, and yes, even our desires. In the beginning of the film we learn that Mother Superior has been talking to God about the need for someone to come and build a chapel. Mother Superior's prayers for her chapel began long before Homer appeared on the scene. We don't know when her prayers began, but we do know that during the course of the movie she not only prayed, but also worked actively to see those prayers answered. We also know that though God answered her prayers in creative and, some might say, miraculous ways, the building was not God's greatest blessing.

Principle Ponderings
1. Like Moses, Homer was in a desert when he came upon the convent. What other similarities are there between Moses and Homer?

2. Mother Superior was intent on having a chapel in her desert community. What is the church and of what is it a symbol? Where is the church?

3. What was Homer's argument for not staying? What was Mother's argument that he should stay and build the chapel? Why do you believe Homer stayed?

Principle Philosophies
1. The church is not the building or the nation. God's people are the church.

2. We are all builders of the church.

3. The purpose of the church is to minister to believers and unbelievers.

Principle Passages

   1. Each generation of the church in each setting has the responsibility of communicating the gospel in understandable terms, considering the language and thought-forms of that setting. —Francis Schaeffer

   2. The mission proper to the church is that of proclaiming the Gospel. —Karl Lehmann

   3. The church is not a gallery for the exhibition of eminent Christians, but a school for the education of imperfect ones. —Henry Ward Beecher

Principle Possibilities

   1. What does building the church today mean in your life?

   2. Are you willing to build the church?

   3. What is it costing you to build the church?

Principle Point ❧

Because he believed in this project, Sidney Poitier agreed to do the movie for less than his normal salary in exchange for a percentage of the profits. He won the Best Actor Academy Award and most likely a bigger paycheck

Chap. 4 — LILIES OF THE FIELD
Study Guide, Week Two, Prayer

Principle Scripture

For we are God's fellow workers; you are God's field, God's building. According to the grace of God given to me, like a skilled master builder I laid a foundation, and another man is building upon it. Let each man take care how he builds upon it
—1 Corinthians 3:9–10

The Prayer Principle

Lilies of the Field is based on a novel of the same title by William E. Barrett. In the novel we learn that there was a fire in the space where the new chapel is to be built. Mother Superior prayed that someone would come along and know exactly what needed to be done so they would have a chapel. Even before Homer agrees to build the chapel he clears away the ruins from the fire. He knew that a strong foundation could not be built on the rubbish. Even more than clearing the plot for the chapel, this shows how various people needed to clean out their own lives in order to be used by God. Homer had to be less prideful, the village priest more humble, and Mr. Ashton, the contractor who delivered the bricks, more generous. Building the church was important, but people becoming more godlike was of even greater importance.

Principle Ponderings

1. Even before Homer agrees to build the chapel what does he do?
2. What does the Bible say about building foundations?
3. What foundations had to be cleared in our lives before we could accept salvation?

Principle Philosophies

1. If you have a strong foundation you can build or rebuild—a church, a family, or a life. But if you've got a weak foundation you can't build anything of lasting value.
2. Hitting rock bottom can actually create a solid foundation on which to rebuild your life.
3. The foundation of a strong life includes our faith, our values, and a sense of purpose.

Principle Passages

1. A belief in God helps provide a foundation to arbitrate our decisions. Without this foundation, we are condemned to live essentially formless lives.
   —Armstrong Williams

2. Do you wish to rise? Begin by descending. You plan a tower that will pierce the clouds? Lay first the foundation of humility. —Saint Augustine

3. I simply can't build my hopes on a foundation of confusion, misery, and death... I think... peace and tranquillity will return again. —Anne Frank

Principle Possibilities

1. How firm are the foundations of your faith, your family, your life?
2. What can you do to shore up a weakened foundation?
3. What frustrations and failures in your life can become the foundation for a stronger faith and a richer life?

Principle Point ℘
In order to get the film made, director Ralph Nelson had to put up his own home as collateral.

Chap. 4 — LILIES OF THE FIELD
Study Guide, Week Three, Prayer

Principle Scripture
Rather, speaking the truth in love, we are to grow up in every way into him who is the head, into Christ, from whom the whole body, joined and knit together by every joint with which it is supplied, when each part is working properly, makes bodily growth and upbuilds itself in love. —Ephesians 4:15–16

The Prayer Principle

Homer takes pride in his efforts, not just pride, but unreasonable pride. Homer decides he can do everything himself and doesn't need any help from anyone. Homer doesn't want help from the villagers. Instead, they sit and watch and wonder why they aren't being asked to use their considerable skills to make their dream come true. Eventually the people get tired of doing nothing and begin to do a little here and a little there. So Homer stomps off to sulk. "I wanted to build it myself. I don't want any help. I wanted to build it myself." Without a leader and a focus, the villagers make many mistakes; and the project begins to fall apart. Finally Homer realizes his role is not to construct the church alone and together they finish the chapel. Homer might have been the contractor, but God was the boss.

Principle Ponderings

1. What tangible tools did Homer have to build the chapel? What intangible tools did he have?
2. What skills did Mother have to get the chapel built?
3. What skills do you have to build your chapel, whether it's a church ministry or reaching others for Christ?

Principle Philosophies

1. Everybody needs a boss, and that should always be God.
2. Just because you aren't the boss doesn't make you less essential.
3. God gave you unique intrinsic gifts to help you build the church.

Principle Passages

1. Sir, my concern is not whether God is on our side; my greatest concern is to be on God's side, for God is always right. —ABRAHAM LINCOLN

2. Prayer does not change God, but it changes the one who prays. —SØREN KIERKEGAARD
3. Prayer is not so much an act as it is an attitude—an attitude of dependency, dependency upon God.
—ARTHUR W. PINK

Principle Possibilities

1. Who is the boss of your life?
2. What's stopping you from allowing God to be boss of your life?
3. How does God want to change you through prayer? Are you willing to be changed?

Principle Point ✺

The movie was filmed in Tucson, Arizona, and the church doors were borrowed from a chapel in Sasabe, Arizona.

Chap. 4 — LILIES OF THE FIELD
Study Guide, Week Four, Prayer

Principle Scripture

Ask, and it will be given you; seek, and you will find; knock, and it will be opened to you. For every one who asks receives, and he who seeks finds, and to him who knocks it will be opened.
—MATTHEW 7:7–8

The Prayer Principle

Framing is where the project becomes more than just an etching on a piece of paper, but a three-dimensional structure. The framing of the chapel was bricks, and they used mortar or grout to hold the bricks together. When Homer ran out of bricks, it looked as if construction would come to a grinding halt. Mother Superior prayed about the bricks, but she also wrote letters asking for donations; and as she wrote, she continued praying. The first step in obtaining what you need is prayer. Like Mother

Superior, you should also be bold and ask for what you need. When God answered Mother's prayers in a surprising way by providing adobe, there was no shortage of adobe and the task was finished. God answers every prayer; he answers yes, no, or wait, and his timing is never wrong.

Principle Ponderings

1. When Mother Superior and the other nuns decided to begin their ministry in the desert many thought they were setting themselves up for failure. What roadblocks did they have?
2. Who are examples of bricks and mortar in the church? Which is more important?
3. Both Homer and Mother Superior were stubborn and believed their way was right. How did they both change? Was the biggest miracle completing the chapel or the change in them and others?

Principle Philosophies

1. Whether you are the brick or the mortar, you are essential to God's plan.
2. Prayer is more than just asking for things.
3. Pray expecting a miracle. God loves to answer prayers in creative ways.

Principle Passages

1. Four steps to achievement: Plan purposefully. Prepare prayerfully. Proceed positively. Pursue persistently.
   —William A. Ward
2. Start by doing what's necessary, then what's possible, and suddenly you are doing the impossible.
   —St. Francis of Assisi

3 When I pray, coincidences happen, and when I don't, they don't. —Sir William Temple

Principle Possibilities

1. Are you putting feet to your prayers in tangible and realistic ways?
2. Are you willing to accept God's answer to your prayers?
3. Instead of focusing on the things you didn't get after praying, are you excited about everything God gave you without asking?

Principle Point ॐ

The movie was shot on location in only fourteen days. The construction crew had to work through the night to keep up with the progress being made on the chapel. Because it was built on rented land, the chapel had to be demolished after filming.

HOPELESS CAUSES

> *Success has nothing to do with what you gain in life or accomplish for yourself. It's what you do for others.* —Danny Thomas

Danny Thomas, star of the hit TV sitcom *Make Room for Daddy*, had a time in his life when his prayers for direction were answered in a way that affected not only his career, but also the lives of tens of thousands of families nationwide.

He believed he had the talent to succeed in the entertainment business, but, like many others, Danny struggled before finding success. The story goes that one day the young entertainer, with a family and only seven dollars in his pocket, got down on his knees in a Detroit church before a statue of St. Jude Thaddeus. He was torn between the need to care for his family and the desire to be in the entertainment business.

"Show me my way in life," prayed Danny Thomas, as he knelt before the patron saint of hopeless causes.

An hour later two offers appeared and he soon moved his family to Chicago to pursue his career. A few years passed and, at another turning point in his life, Danny once again prayed to St. Jude for answers, but this time with a twist. As he prayed for answers he pledged to one day build a shrine to the saint.

Within the next year Danny was earning $500 a week at the 5100 Club in Chicago, and the rest, as they say, is history. Over the years Danny went from being almost penniless to becoming one of the most successful and beloved entertainers of all time.

Many people make desperate promises only to forget them when their fortunes turn. During the years his career flourished Danny remembered his pledge and the idea of building a children's hospital became his dream. With Memphis, Tennessee, as the eventual site, Danny began tapping friends and contacts to help raise the funds to create a unique research hospital devoted to curing catastrophic diseases in children.

Thanks to his vision, entertainers willing to make the trek to Memphis to perform and fundraise, and local business leaders, by the mid 1950s it seemed the needed funds were in place to build the hospital. But that was just the first step. Before the hospital could be built a plan had to be made to ensure consistent funds for the annual operating budget.

Born into a family of Lebanese immigrants, Danny Thomas believed that Arabic-speaking Americans owed a debt of gratitude to the United States for the gifts of freedom given their parents. In 1957, Danny convinced a hundred representatives of the Arab-American community to form the American Lebanese Syrian Associated Charities (ALSAC) for the purpose of raising funds for St. Jude Children's Research Hospital. In 1962 Danny's promise of a shrine to St. Jude became a reality when St. Jude Children's Research Hospital opened its doors.

Danny Thomas gave millions of Americans the gift of laughter through his acting and as a successful television producer working on many popular shows including *The Dick Van Dyke Show*, *The Andy Griffith Show*, and *The Mod Squad*. More important in the grand scheme of things is that his prayer for direction and subsequent promise to build a shrine to St. Jude led to the building of what has become a beacon of hope for the catastrophically ill children of the world.

—FIVE—

Principle Scripture
Whatever your task, work heartily, as serving the Lord and not men. —Colossians 3:23

The Transformative Power of
PRACTICE

Akeelah and the Bee

THE GREATEST ORATOR

> *Practice does not make perfect.*
> *Only perfect practice makes perfect.*
> —Vince Lombardi

All his life Winston Churchill had a speech impediment that would stop most people from choosing a career in politics. Instead of failing, Churchill was considered the best orator in Parliament despite the fact that he was a stutterer. His success can be summed up in two words: "practice" and "believe."

Before he returned to India as an officer in the British Army, Churchill sought help from Sir Felix Semen, a speech specialist who was also Physician-in-Ordinary to the Court. He told Churchill that what he had was no actual defect and that his speech impediment stemmed from his fear of not being able to answer intelligently when asked a question. He advised the young man to practice to overcome his fears.

The future prime minister took the doctor's suggestion to heart and began practicing tongue twisters. He also made sure he would never be caught unawares when speaking, and in this way he could avoid his stutter. Churchill, who was known for his witty retorts and well thought out arguments, spent hours studying a topic and writing answers to any question he might be asked, days or sometimes weeks in advance. He so believed

AKEELAH AND THE BEE

in his ability to become a great statesman that he memorized his writings forward and backward and practiced them until he no longer stuttered.

Unlike Winston Churchill, in *Akeelah and the Bee* eleven-year-old Akeelah is not afraid to speak or spell, but, like Churchill, she discovers the value of practicing for the National Spelling Bee. In this heartwarming movie Akeelah not only learns that practice makes perfect, but that there are more important things in life than winning.

Changing the world . . . one word at a time.

prac•tice. *noun.* **To do or perform (something) repeatedly in order to acquire or polish a skill**

"If you want to be good, you have to practice, practice, practice. If you don't love something, then don't do it," said author Ray Bradbury. It's not enough to know your purpose or set priorities if you're not willing to practice. In this chapter we look at how practicing is one way we show that we believe in ourselves and often in those around us.

Synopsis

Being blessed with great potential is usually not enough to achieve great things in life, and that is where our story begins. The first voice we hear is that of Keke Palmer in the role of eleven-year-old Akeelah Anderson. Her potential was such that before her father was killed in a random drive-by shooting, she skipped second grade. Instead of blossoming, however, her academic promise is choking in the weeds of underachievement.

"You know that feeling that no matter what you do or where you go you just don't fit in? Don't know the word for that. 'Alienation.' 'Estrangement.' 'Incompatibility.' Nah, those aren't right. But there's got to be a word for it, cause that's how I feel all the time."

In an effort to fit into her dilapidated school in South Central Los Angeles, Akeelah has resorted to skipping classes and deliberately getting bad grades so she is not labeled a "brainiac." Her overworked mother (Angela Bassett) has her hands full with three siblings, one already running with the wrong crowd, another a teen mother. Akeelah would have achieved her goal of blending in had it not been for one thing: spelling.

Akeelah can spell. It's not a skill that she has cultivated on purpose. Without realizing it she has learned that spelling calms her down, makes her happy, and, best of all, connects her to her late father.

After getting yet another embarrassing perfect score on the weekly spelling test, her teacher suggests that she compete in the first annual school spelling bee. Her first reaction is to say no. However when given the choice between detentions for missing so much school or the spelling bee, Akeelah wisely chooses the latter and sets her destiny into motion.

The principal invites Dr. Larabee (Laurence Fishburne), a UCLA professor and former spelling champ, to attend, and Akeelah easily outspells her opponents. Dr. Larabee is impressed with Akeelah's memory, but doesn't think she has the discipline to make it to the National Bee in Washington, D.C. At first he turns her away, unimpressed with her attitude and ghetto talk, but she stubbornly overcomes his objections.

Her journey to Washington, D.C., takes place over an entire school year. During this time we meet Javier and Dylan, two young men who eventually believe in Akeelah and play a pivotal role in Akeelah's growth as a speller and ultimately as a person of character.

Dr. Larabee teaches her that the National Spelling Bee isn't a game and requires an enormous of amount of practice. Her coach teaches her about word construction, etymologies, and mnemonic tricks. As he continues to coach Akeelah, he helps her to understand that the willingness to win is more important than knowing how to win.

At one point Akeelah reads a quote often erroneously credited to Nelson Mandela but actually written by Marianne

Williamson: "Our deepest fear is not that we are inadequate. Our deepest fear is that we are powerful beyond measure. We ask ourselves, 'Who am I to be brilliant? gorgeous? talented? fabulous?' Actually, who are you not to be? We were born to make manifest the glory of God that is within us. And as we let our own light shine, we unconsciously give other people permission to do the same."

As she comes to understand the quote, she realizes that she must believe in herself and allow others to believe. Akeelah doesn't just want to win. She must win. Knowing that she was uniquely made by God to spell, to let her light shine, gives Akeelah the courage to do something extraordinary.

When Akeelah qualifies for the nationals in Washington, D.C. Dr. Larabee tells her he has taught her all that he can. He gives her four boxes of vocabulary cards so she can practice on her own. Akeelah is devastated and shares with her mother about the loss of her coach at such a critical time.

"You ain't short on people who want to help you," reasons her mother. "I bet if you look around you got fifty thousand coaches, starting with me."

One of the most heart-warming parts of the movie is when Akeelah discovers her mother's statement about fifty thousand coaches in the neighborhood is true. When word spreads that she needs to practice if she is to have a shot at winning, the entire neighborhood lends support. Soon her family, friends, and neighbors from all walks of life are quizzing her. The entire community believes that she can win the National Spelling Bee.

The climax comes at the National Spelling Bee in a way no one expected. Akeelah, Javier, and Dylan make it into the top five before Javier misses a word. Finally, only Akeelah and Dylan are left standing and the judges call a short break before the two adversaries face off with the championship words.

During a break Akeelah hears Dylan's father warning him that if he loses to "that girl" he will be second place for the rest of his life. By now Akeelah has a legion of people who believe in her for all the right reasons, while Dylan seems to have only his father who believes he can win, even if the process of winning brings him no joy.

Dylan realizes that Akeelah has deliberately misspelled a word so that he can win, so he also stumbles on a word he obviously knows. He asks for water and takes the opportunity to confront Akeelah. Her reasoning is that she has two more years and this is his last opportunity. Dylan demands that Akeelah do her best to beat him. He knows the meaning of the word "honor" and doesn't want to finish in first place unless he has won it fairly.

The two tenacious spellers return to the stage. Akeelah and Dylan battle for the title and, after exhausting every championship word, they share the title for the first time in the history of the National Spelling Bee. As the audience, both in the auditorium and those watching television back home, erupts into cheers, we hear Akeelah's last words.

"You know that feeling where everything feels right? Where you don't have to worry about tomorrow or yesterday, where you feel safe and know you're doing the best you can? There's a word for that, it's called love. L-O-V-E. And it's what I feel for all my family and all my coaches. In my neighborhood. Where I come from. Where I learned how to spell."

Chap. 5 — AKEELAH AND THE BEE
Study Guide, Week One, Practice

Principle Scripture
I can do all things through him who strengthens me.

—Philippians 4:13

AKEELAH AND THE BEE

The Practice Principle

There is an inborn hunger in all humans to find kindred spirits, and Akeelah is no different than anyone else. In a voiceover Akeelah talks about trying to find just the right word to describe how she feels all of the time. She rules out "alienation," "estrangement," and "incompatibility," but we know what she means. Jeremiah 29:11 reminds us that the Lord knows the plans that are in store for us, plans for welfare and not for evil, to give us a future and a hope. Practicing her gift and developing her strengths help Akeelah succeed and ultimately influence others. Sometimes God's plans play out differently, and so much better, than we could ever imagine.

Principle Ponderings

1. What happened to smart kids at Akeelah's school? What were they called when they got a good grade on a test? Even though she was smart, Akeelah wanted to be like everyone else and not stand out. How did she try to achieve that goal?
2. Was she using the gifts God gave her? Was she fulfilled?
3. What were the principal's motives for pushing Akeelah to compete in the school bee? What good came out of her participation?

Principle Philosophies

1. Everyone has a special gift. The trick is to find it and then to have the courage to use it.
2. Someone once said that being green isn't easy. Would we really want a world where everyone was blue?
3. Don't fear standing out. Strive to be fearlessly outstanding.

Principle Passages Practice

1. Artistic talent is a gift from God and whoever discovers it in himself has a certain obligation: to know that he cannot waste this talent, but must develop it.
   —Pope John Paul II

2. Hide not your talents, they for use were made, what's a sundial in the shade? —Benjamin Franklin

3. When I stand before God at the end of my life, I would hope that I would not have a single bit of talent left, and could say, "I used everything you gave me."
   —Erma Bombeck

Principle Possibilities

1. If you could set aside your fears and the expectations of what others would think of you, what would you love to do with your life?

2. When trying to determine your special gift, ask yourself what you are drawn to? What can you learn or do easily? What brings you joy?

3. What gifts are you not using? Why? Could God use you more effectively if you worked toward fulfilling your potential?

Principle Point ✽

Akeelah and the Bee was the first film produced by Starbucks.

Chap. 5 — AKEELAH AND THE BEE
Study Guide, Week Two, Practice

Principle Scripture

For God did not give us a spirit of timidity but a spirit of power and love and self-control. —2 Timothy 1:7

The Practice Principle

After Akeelah wins the school Bee, her principal arranges to have Dr. Larabee consider coaching her. She arrives late for their appointment and things get worse from there. He calls her out for being insolent and using street language. It's obvious that Akeelah and Dr. Larabee are both intelligent and stubborn yet somehow they manage to work together. Dr. Larabee understands that Akeelah must not only memorize words. She must be diligent in her ability to understand word construction, etymologies, and mnemonic tricks. Because he believes in her abilities, he must instil in his prodigy the need for discipline.

Principle Ponderings

1. Although Akeelah had natural talents in spelling, what did it require for her to polish her strengths and become a real champion?

2. Akeelah failed at spelling a word on more than one occasion. What did she learn from her failures?

3. How do you think her newly acquired discipline helped Akeelah in the future?

Principle Philosophies

1. Discipline is freedom because it allows you to succeed in ways others can only dream of.

2. Becoming disciplined is easier when you have a goal.

3. Discipline often requires new behaviors.

Principle Passages

1. It doesn't matter what you're trying to accomplish. It's all a matter of discipline. —Wilma Rudolph

2. Discipline is the bridge between goals and accomplishment. —Jim Rohn

3 Discipline is the refining fire by which talent becomes ability. —Roy L. Smith

Principle Possibilities

1. Has anyone ever pushed you to do something that you yourself did not think you could do? What did you learn from the experience?

2. Proverbs 16:3 says to commit your work to the Lord, and your plans will be established. Do you have a success plan in place to increase your discipline in specific areas?

3. What have you learned from your failures that helped in other endeavors?

Principle Point ❧

Akeelah and the Bee was filmed in thirty-one days. The budget was a mere six million dollars.

Chap. 5 — AKEELAH AND THE BEE
Study Guide, Week Three, Practice

Principle Scripture
Iron sharpens iron, and one man sharpens the wits of another.
—Proverbs 27:17

The Practice Principle
Each of the three spelling bee contenders has varying levels of support during their quest. Javier's parents are loving and supportive. Dylan comes from a completely different background, where winning is everything and losing is unacceptable. Akeelah's mother is unsupportive for a large part of the movie. After realizing that Akeelah is serious about the Bee, her mother shares the fear she has for her daughter. Instead of seeing one winner on the video she saw two hundred losers, and she didn't want that for Akeelah. Sometimes the difference between winning and losing is the support you have or the support you offer to others.

Principle Ponderings

1. What did Akeelah and Dr. Larabee each gain from working together? Who gained the most?
2. Dr. Larabee gave Akeelah the tools for success, but she still needed encouragement and support to face the competition from the experienced and privileged students. Where did she find the support she needed? What did her "coaches" gain from the experience of helping Akeelah?
3. Support can be found in the most unlikely places. Who was Akeelah's surprise coach?

Principle Philosophies

1. If others don't recognize or affirm your strengths, remember that God does.
2. Your mastery of a unique skill can empower others.
3. If you look around, there are always people willing to help in the role of a teacher, mentor, tutor, or coach.

Principle Passages

1. I realized that God has placed Christians everywhere, to support each other, to support the needy in those areas, and that is the thing that I find is a great plus.
   —Cliff Richard
2. What do we live for if not to make life less difficult for each other? —George Eliot
3. In this world we must help one another.
   —Jean de la Fontaine

Principle Possibilities

1. Working with others can be challenging and sometimes confrontational. How have you handled a particularly

challenging or confrontational person or situation? Did you grow spiritually as a result?

2. Was there ever a time when you quit because of not having support? Does the memory of that time encourage you to help others?

3. Where do you find support? How can you be more supportive of those around you?

Principle Point ✤
Dr. Larabee is based on the director's teacher, Mr. Larabelle.

Chap. 5 — AKEELAH AND THE BEE
Study Guide, Week Four, Practice

Principle Scripture
Do not be conformed to this world but be transformed by the renewal of your mind, that you may prove what is the will of God, what is good and acceptable and perfect. —Romans 12:2

The Practice Principle
When Akeelah and Dylan are the only competitors left, Akeelah makes a decision to let Dylan win. Her reasoning is that she has two more years, and this is his last opportunity. Dylan demands that Akeelah do her best to beat him. When she reminds him about his father's intense desire for Dylan to win, he points out that his father "has never won anything in his life" and lives through Dylan's accomplishments. He knows the meaning of the word "honor" and doesn't want to finish in first place unless he has won it fairly.

In the end, both Akeelah and Dylan lived out the final part of the Marianne Williamson quote featured in the movie. "We were born to make manifest the glory of God that is within us. And as we let our own light shine, we unconsciously give other people permission to do the same."

AKEELAH AND THE BEE

Principle Ponderings

1. Akeelah forges her father's signature, takes a bus to a study group without permission, and lies about summer school. Do we see a change in her character over time?
2. At the district bee, one of the students and his mother cheat when spelling his last word. What do you think drives people to cheat? What is it that brings about the need to win no matter the cost?
3. Philippians 2:3 says to "do nothing from rivalry or conceit, but in humility count others more significant than yourselves." Do you think Akeelah's head-to-head with Dylan exemplified the scripture?

Principle Philosophies

1. Every day you have countless opportunities to show others your Christlike character.
2. Making a mistake in how you handle a situation once does not mean you can never make amends.
3. Winning is usually the least important thing in becoming the person God wants us to be.

Principle Passages

1. It was character that got us out of bed, commitment that moved us into action, and discipline that enabled us to follow through. —ZIG ZIGLAR
2. Knowledge will give you power, but character respect. —BRUCE LEE
3. The discipline you learn and character you build from setting and achieving a goal can be more valuable than the achievement of the goal itself. —BO BENNET

Principle Possibilities

1. What goal in your life will make you work as hard as Akeelah did?
2. How does your faith affect the way you deal with obstacles or trials?
3. Was there ever a time when you exhibited bad character to get what you wanted? Did you admit it to yourself or others and work to make it right?

Principle Point ೞ

Sidney Poitier was first considered for the role of Dr. Larabee. They decided to go with someone younger, and Laurence Fishburne won the role.

THE MVP OF PRACTICE

> *You have to expect things of yourself before you can do them.*
> —Michael Jordan

Even if you are not an avid basketball fan you can't help but know that Michael Jordan is one of the greatest basketball players of all time. As with any legend, truths and untruths abound, and sometimes it's hard to know what to believe. One of the stories surrounding Jordan's potential as a student athlete was that he had been cut from his high school basketball team.

Growing up in Wilmington, North Carolina, Jordan played baseball and football in addition to the sport where his potential eventually shone. The already five-feet ten-inch tenth grader became the quarterback for the Laney High School junior varsity team. That could have been where Michael Jordan made his mark had it not been for a case of sibling rivalry. Jordan's older brother, Larry, routinely beat him in one-on-one basketball games, fuelling the younger Jordan's competitive streak and moving him off the gridiron and onto the court.

It's hard to believe that Coach Clifton Herring didn't believe in the young man who would later define professional basketball. In a *Sports Illustrated* article Herring explained that Jordan wasn't cut from the team; he just wasn't given the opportunity to play on the varsity squad.

Herring absolutely saw his potential and believed in the young Jordan, but he also believed that the varsity should be reserved for upperclassmen. Jordan, as a sophomore, was automatically relegated to the junior varsity squad. Imagine Jordan's frustration when he looked at the team list and discovered a sophomore's name and it wasn't his. The omission had nothing to do with the coach not recognizing Jordan's potential and everything to do with height.

The varsity team lacked a big man that year and at six feet five inches to Jordan's five feet ten inches, his teammate Leroy Smith made the team, leaving Jordan upset and determined to never be left off a team again. Michael practiced harder than ever on his basketball skills, eventually leading to a college scholarship, an Olympic gold medal, the NBA Rookie of the Year Award, five regular-season MVPs, three All-Star MVPs, and six NBA championship rings with the Chicago Bulls.

Michael Jordan has come a long way from the teenager crying in his bedroom over not making the team. He obviously had potential, but it was the combination of that potential and practice that put Jordan on the road to becoming the most decorated player in the NBA. "I've missed more than nine thousand shots in my career," explained Jordan when sharing the secret to his success. "I've lost almost three hundred games. Twenty-six times I've been trusted to take the game-winning shot and missed. I've failed over and over and over again in my life. And that is why I succeed."

Most of us will never be a Michael Jordan in our endeavors, but perceived shortcomings and failures can drive us to believe in practice to reach our full potential.

—SIX—

Principle Scripture
You need to persevere so that when you have done the will of God, you will receive what he has promised. —Hebrews 10:36

The Transformative Power of
PERSEVERANCE

Under the Same Moon

KEY BY KEY, STEP BY STEP

> *I do not think that there is any other quality so essential to success of any kind as the quality of perseverance. It overcomes almost everything, even nature.* —John D. Rockefeller

Author Orison Swett Marden could have been referencing Paul Smith when he said, "Success is not measured by what you accomplish but by the opposition you have encountered, and the courage with which you have maintained the struggle against overwhelming odds." This little-known man who persevered was born in 1921 in Philadelphia and diagnosed with severe spastic cerebral palsy as a child. Because of his condition communication was an enormous challenge; he couldn't feed himself, tie his shoes, or do the myriad other everyday activities we all take for granted. He was unable to attend school and never learned to read or write, but he had a gift that helped with the pain of being different from those around him.

He refused to be defined by his cerebral palsy, and Paul not only lived, which had been in doubt, but he thrived. It took fifteen years for him to learn how to speak and thirty-two to learn

UNDER THE SAME MOON

to walk, but his perseverance paid off. He excelled at chess and became a master artist even though he could not hold a paintbrush or use his hands in a significant way.

When he was fifteen Paul started using a typewriter to craft art using his left hand to steady the right. Because he could not type with both hands, he locked the "shift" key and began to create works of art using the @ # $ % ^ & * ( ) and _ keys. For two or three hours each day Paul listened to classical music while working hard at his typewriter art. Each piece took between two weeks and three months to complete.

Overcoming obstacles we cannot even imagine, by perseverance Paul became one of the most acclaimed typewriter artists in history. With great effort Paul began to smudge the typewritten letters to produce subtle shadings and textures creating art that resembled charcoal and pencil drawings. Color typewriter ribbons gave Paul the opportunity to go beyond his black and white masterpieces. Despite his pain and physical limitations, Paul produced original works of art as well as copies of masterpieces. In 2004, because of worsening cataracts, Paul stopped making his typewriter art. He believed that gifts must be shared, and though he left behind a portfolio of his art, he gave most of his collection away. He died in 2007 at the Oregon nursing facility he called home.

Like Paul Smith, in the movie *Under the Same Moon* Carlitos perseveres against all odds. He could easily walk and talk, but the obstacle of leaving Mexico on a search for his mother somewhere in Los Angeles would have daunted adults, let alone a nine-year-old boy.

Australian surveyor Edward Counsel once said that there is no thornless path in this world, and I am sure Paul Smith would agree. His path was filled with the pain of overcoming thorny obstacles, but his artwork is a reminder that if we believe in ourselves with perseverance we can overcome anything in life. Carlitos's path was no less thorny as he dodged immigration officers, police, and people who wanted to do him harm.

In the end, both Paul and Carlitos believed and persevered and changed their lives.

> *The love between a mother and son
> knows no boundaries.*

per•se•ver•ance. *noun.* Steadfastness in doing something despite difficulty or delay in achieving success

Perseverance is a positive, active characteristic, and as Charles Spurgeon reminds us, "by perseverance the snail reached the ark." *Under the Same Moon* tells a parallel story of a mother who immigrates illegally to the United States and Carlitos, her nine-year-old son, who lives in Mexico waiting for her to earn enough to send for him. We can't sit idly, passively waiting and hoping for some good thing to happen. This chapter helps us to discover what God has placed in us to help us to persevere during difficult times.

Synopsis

Under the Same Moon tells the story of Rosario (Kate del Castillo), a mother who illegally immigrates to the United States, and her nine-year-old son, Carlitos (Adrian Alonso). Carlitos's father abandoned the two soon after his son's birth, and for the past four years Rosario has been working two jobs as an undocumented domestic in a wealthy Los Angeles gated community. Every Sunday she calls her son from a payphone and paints a word picture of her neighborhood surroundings, promising her only child that one day soon they will be together. She reminds him that when he gets tired of persevering to remember that when they go to bed at night they are both sleeping under the same moon.

When his grandmother dies in her sleep, Carlitos decides that he can't live with his aunt and uncle, who want him only because of the three hundred dollars his mother sends for his care each month. He is determined to see his mother before her next Sunday call and decides to cross the border with the help of a young couple who transport children illegally for profit. They successfully cross the border with Carlitos, but their car is flagged for unpaid tickets, impounded, and towed away. Carlitos manages to get out of the car but is separated from the couple and continues his journey alone.

Turning back is not an option so he perseveres and eventually finds a community of illegal immigrants and stays with them picking tomatoes. The immigration police raid the building, and Carlitos and another worker named Enrique (Eugenio Derbez) become new traveling companions.

During their journey Carlitos tries to bond with Enrique, who has no interest in being a nursemaid to a nine-year-old kid. Besides, his final destination is New York not Los Angeles. Little by little the unlikely pair grow closer and Carlitos finds a dishwashing job at a diner in Arizona on the condition that Enrique also gets to work. Enrique encourages Carlitos to find and call his birthfather with information Carlitos gleaned from his uncle before leaving.

Over a hamburger paid for by Carlitos, his father, Oscar, promises to take him to Los Angeles, but the following morning he fails to arrive at the diner to begin the trip. Enrique, who has begun to feel responsible for Carlitos, decides to take him to Los Angeles.

The drama cuts between Carlitos's dangerous week-long journey and Rosario's difficult life including being fired after demanding the pay her boss has withheld knowing that as an illegal she cannot complain to the authorities. In the midst of her challenges she learns that Carlitos has gone across the border and has not been seen since. Not knowing her son is already in Los Angeles she decides she must take a bus back to Mexico in search of her lost son.

Carlitos has only Rosario's post office box address, so he and Enrique search for the payphone his mother uses each Sunday morning at ten o'clock. For four years Rosario has described her surroundings including a Laundromat, a pizzeria, and a mural somewhere in East Los Angeles. After searching for hours the two weary travelers fall asleep on a park bench.

As the sun rises Carlitos is still sleeping on a park bench, and Enrique leaves to buy food. Carlitos, a little boy alone, is spotted and almost caught by the police. Enrique, who shows up just in time, throws a cup of coffee at the officers so the police chase him instead. Carlitos manages to escape, but Enrique is caught. He knows that without papers he will most likely be deported, but Enrique is willing to sacrifice himself to save his young friend.

Carlitos runs away and finds himself near a payphone. He glances around and sees a Laundromat, a pizzeria, and the mural his mother has described. Even more miraculous is the fact that Rosario has decided to make one more call and goes to the phone she has been using every Sunday for four years. She is finally reunited with Carlitos.

Under the Same Moon shows us the bond between a mother and her son and the perseverance it takes to be together against all odds.

Chap. 6 — UNDER THE SAME MOON
Study Guide, Week One, Perseverance

Principle Scripture
So faith, hope, love abide, these three; but the greatest of these is love. —1 Corinthians 13:13

The Perseverance Principle
Nine-year-old Carlitos wants to go home. Not to a physical place, but as he defines home: wherever his mother is. The heartbreak of illegal immigration is the cornerstone of this poignant movie. When Carlitos tires of waiting for their reunion, his mother reminds him that when they both go to bed each night they are still sleeping under the same moon. The political issue of illegal immigration is ever-present, but *Under the Same*

Moon is an unforgettable story of the invincible bond between a mother and son.

Principle Ponderings

1. Love is at the heart of the movie. How did various characters show their love during the course of the movie?
2. Carlitos had a place to live, his needs were met, and he could have continued waiting for his mother to bring him to Los Angeles. What caused him to decide to leave?
3. Did all the characters behave in a selfless way? If not, who didn't and what was their motive?

Principle Philosophies

1. There is no substitute for a mother's love.
2. Loving someone gives you courage for the journey.
3. We can live without love, but what an empty life it would be.

Principle Passages

1. The relationship between mother and son has no nationality. —Ligiah Villalobos
2. A little girl, asked where her home was, replied, "Where mother is." —Keith L. Brooks
3. She never quite leaves her children at home, even when she doesn't take them along.
   —Margaret Culkin Banning

Principle Possibilities

1. What have you done to stay connected with your family even when it was difficult?

2. Various characters express love in many different ways in the movie. Whether they are friends or strangers, do any of these expressions make you consider how you love others? In what way?

3. Do you feel so loved that God would chase you to the ends of the earth to wrap his arms around you and bring you home?

Principle Point 💫
Director Patricia Riggen was born in Guadalajara, Jalisco, educated in Mexico, and got her master's in screenwriting at Columbia University.

Chap. 6 — UNDER THE SAME MOON
Study Guide, Week Two Perseverance

Principle Scripture
And be kind to one another, tenderhearted, forgiving one another, as God in Christ has forgiven you. —EPHESIANS 4:32

The Perseverance Principle
Under the Same Moon puts human faces on the divisive issue of illegal immigrants, particularly those coming north from Mexico. The story tells of the heartbreaking reality of many families torn apart by borders, but it also shows the goodness and hospitality of many people Carlitos meets along the way.

Principle Ponderings
1. Why did Martha and David (the two coyotes) go over the border? Did they care about Carlitos and his plight?

2. Were there any illegal immigrants who helped Carlitos on his journey? Did any people not in danger of being deported help?

3. Who was kind to Rosario? Did she respond to his kindness or believe it was done out of goodness without wanting something in return?

Principle Philosophies

1. Life's race is never a straight path. But it's the twists and turns that take us places we never imagined.
2. Live life so that you are closer to your goal today than you were yesterday.
3. We become kind by being kind.

Principle Passages

1. With ordinary talent and extraordinary perseverance, all things are attainable. —THOMAS FOXWELL BUXTON
2. Saints are sinners who kept on going.
 —ROBERT LOUIS STEVENSON
3. No act of kindness, no matter how small, is ever wasted.
 —AESOP

Principle Possibilities

1. After watching *Under the Same Moon* were your attitudes about the immigration issue changed? If so, how?
2. As a Christian what do you think is the right response to illegal immigrants and the overall issue of immigration? Do you think God is calling you to become involved in the issue?
3. During the film we see the kindness of strangers at work. Are you kind to illegal immigrants and others that many in your community see as undesirable? What can you personally do to make a difference?

Principle Point ✥
Adrian Alonso (Carlitos) learned English on the set while starring in *The Legend of Zorro* in 2005.

Chap. 6 — UNDER THE SAME MOON
Study Guide, Week Three, Perseverance

Principle Scripture
More than that, we rejoice in our sufferings, knowing that suffering produces endurance, and endurance produces character, and character produces hope, and hope does not disappoint us, because God's love has been poured into our hearts through the Holy Spirit which has been given to us. —Romans 5:3–5

The Persevernce Principle
Both Carlitos and his mother went through trials as they worked toward their goal of being together. Rosario's employer withholds her money knowing she cannot complain, as she has no papers to legally be in the United States. Carlitos loses his money as he flees from the impounded car and, as a result, he falls into the wrong crowd that tries to sell him to another man, possibly for sexual purposes. Miraculously Reyna, the owner of a local safe house for illegal workers, helps him. Reyna is the first example of selfless sacrifice, putting herself in danger by helping Carlitos and spending a hundred dollars in the process. Because of those who sacrificed, Carlitos' is able to persevere.

Principle Ponderings

1. In addition to Reyna, who else would you say sacrificed for either Carlitos or Rosario?

2. In what ways did Enrique sacrifice during the journey?

3. Who would you say is the Jesus character in the movie and why?

UNDER THE SAME MOON

Principle Philosophies

1. The difference between average and extraordinary people is the willingness to sacrifice.
2. There are struggles in everyone's life, but the more we sacrifice for others the less pain we seem to have.
3. When we compare Jesus' sacrifice to what we can do for others, how can we not do the right thing?

Principle Passages

1. A man who was completely innocent offered himself as a sacrifice for the good of others, including his enemies, and became the ransom of the world. It was a perfect act. —MAHATMA GANDHI
2. Great achievement is usually born of great sacrifice, and is never the result of selfishness. —NAPOLEON HILL
3. No one has greater love than this, to lay down one's life for one's friends. —JOHN 15:13

Principle Possibilities

1. Have you ever had to sacrifice something for the ones you love? What were those things? Did your sacrifices eventually help those people you were trying to help?
2. Did someone ever make an unbelievable sacrifice for you? What was it and how did that make you feel?
3. Do you feel that the sacrifices you make are required of you by God or done by you because of God's plan for your life?

Principle Point ❧

The $2 million Spanish language film started a bidding war at the 2007 Sundance Film Festival. When it was released nationwide it earned $2.7 million from only 266 theaters opening weekend, eventually bringing in close to $13 million in fewer than six months.

Chap. 6 — UNDER THE SAME MOON
Study Guide, Week Four, Perseverance

Principle Scripture

Blessed is the man who endures trial, for when he has stood the test he will receive the crown of life which God has promised to those who love him. —JAMES 1:12

The Perseverance Principle

With a lot of perseverance, help from friends and strangers, serendipity, and a sprinkle of Hollywood magic, Carlitos finally finds his mother. The tale is poignant, in turn both heartbreaking and heartwarming. The bond between Carlitos and Rosario never lessens. However, the relationship between Carlitos and Enrique adds another dimension and gives viewers some much needed comic relief to balance the harshness of what life is like for immigrants trying to enter the country without proper identification. The growing bond between Enrique and Carlitos helps us to understand that friendship and hope can come from the most unlikely source. It also helps us to remember that, when we hold on to God's word, good triumphs over bad.

Principle Ponderings

1. The story ends with Carlitos and his mother finally together in Los Angeles but still illegal. What lessons did they both learn that would help them as they continue to become citizens?

2. Do you think that now that her son is with her she will marry Paco? If so, do you think she is settling because life has been so difficult.

3. How does Carlitos's journey parallel our life journey?

Principle Philosophies

1. When your head says, "Give up," your heart whispers, "Try it one more time."
2. Never think that God's delays are God's denials.
3. In the end love conquers all.

Principle Passages

1. Perseverance is not a long race; it is many short races one after another. —Walter Elliott
2. Dreams do come true if we only wish hard enough. You can have anything in life if you will sacrifice everything else for it. —James M. Barrie
3. Look at a stonecutter hammering away at his rock, perhaps a hundred times without as much as a crack showing in it. Yet at the hundred-and-first blow it will split in two, and I know it was not the last blow that did it, but all that had gone before. —Jacob A. Riis

Principle Possibilities

1. Is there a journey you are on right now that has you wanting to give up or turn back? What will it take for you to persevere?
2. It's the small pebbles that cause you to trip on life's journey, not the mountain. What spiritual pebbles are you tripping over as you make your way to the mountain called heaven?
3. Do you have friends who have appeared along the way who have helped you during a spiritual, emotional, or physical crisis? Do you believe they are there by accident or by God's design?

Principle Point ❧
When Rosario is seen marking a date off on her calendar, she says, in Spanish, "Carlitos' Cumple" as she writes. There are no apostrophes preceding an "s" in Spanish, and the date that she used to show Carlitos's upcoming birthday should have read "Cumple de Carlitos."

THE STOLEN GENERATIONS

> *The most essential factor is persistence —*
> *the determination never to allow your*
> *energy or enthusiasm to be dampened*
> *by the discouragement that must*
> *inevitably come.*
> —JAMES WHITCOMB RILEY

What if you were stolen from your family for the most heinous of reasons? And what if your home lay almost one thousand miles away? Would you do anything to get back to your family? That is exactly what happened to three young girls who practiced perseverance in a quest to return to their homeland against staggering odds.

In 1931 Molly Kelly, a fourteen-year-old Aboriginal girl, her eight-year-old sister, Daisy, and their ten-year-old cousin, Gracie, were taken away from their families in Jigalong, Australia in the belief that part-Aboriginal children should be trained as domestic servants. Between 1909 and 1969 more than a hundred thousand children were taken from their families as part of the official government policy of forced removal of Aboriginals so that they could be merged into the white community. The policy was designed to "assimilate" or "breed out" indigenous people. These children became known as the "Stolen Generations."

After one day in Moore River, the three girls escaped and began their long journey home. Molly decided that since

Jigalong was along the rabbit-proof fence line that ran through Western Australia, if they headed east from Moore River to the fence and then north, they could find their home. The three girls crossed a flooded river, sand dunes, red dust country, a salt lake, and more during their nine-week journey. They slept in rabbit burrows, caught and cooked rabbits, and ate wild sweet potatoes and bananas as they evaded their captors.

Outraged that three half-caste girls had the audacity to run away, A. O. Neville, the Chief Protector of Aborigines in the State of Western Australia, hired an Aboriginal tracker to find them. However, Molly persevered.

Sadly, Gracie believed the lie that Neville spread about her mother waiting for her. When the little girl tried to get home on her own by finding the train station, Gracie was recaptured. Molly and Daisy persisted and, after their unimaginable journey through the Outback, the two sisters made it home and went into hiding in the desert with their mother and grandmother.

Despite her courage and perseverance Molly displayed on her trek back to her mother, there wasn't a happy ending. Nine years later, authorities transported Molly and her two daughters, eighteen-month-old Annabelle, and four-year-old Doris, back to Moore River. Molly was able to escape with Annabelle, but later the government removed Annabelle from Molly's care and they never saw each other again. Doris, however, was reunited with Molly in the 1960s and chronicled her mother's daring escape in her book *Follow the Rabbit-Proof Fence*, which was the basis for the 2002 film *Rabbit-Proof Fence*. The pull toward family and home made Molly persevere.

—SEVEN—

Principle Scripture

He will wipe away every tear from their eyes, and death shall be no more, neither shall there be mourning nor crying nor pain any more, for the former things have passed away.

—Revelation 21:4

The Transformative Power of
PAIN

We Are Marshall

TEARS IN HEAVEN

> *Tears are often the telescope*
> *by which men see far into heaven.*
> —Henry Ward Beecher

In his song "Tears in Heaven" Eric Clapton has written a powerful message about death and those left behind. At the 1993 Grammy Awards, "Tears in Heaven" received the Grammy as the Song of the Year. The album that contained it won Album of the Year, and Mr. Clapton himself was applauded as Male Vocalist of the Year.

Fans around the world grieved with the family when they learned that the singer's four-year-old son had fallen to his death from a fifty-third floor New York City apartment building. In a few moving moments, Clapton acknowledges that death, sings of the assurance that his son is in heaven, and admits his grief and the need to be strong. Although the song is obviously filled with despair, the chorus affirms that there is hope. This tribute, with the haunting refrain, offers us a ray of sunshine when it insists there will be no tears in heaven.

WE ARE MARSHALL

Clapton would love to rest in heaven with his son, but he knows it is not yet his time, and he will have to carry his own sorrow. The hope that he sings of is in the future for himself and the present for his little boy.

Like Clapton, the town of Huntington, West Virginia, has that same hope in *We Are Marshall*. Eric Clapton honored his son by using his gifts to write a song that has given great comfort to those who are in tremendous pain, and the new football team honored their teammates by rebuilding the program.

We Are Marshall tells the moving, true story of the men who work to rebuild the Thundering Herd varsity football team after a tragic plane crash in November 1970. The emotional pain of losing virtually the entire football team and coaching staff nearly destroys the Marshall University football program, but the newly hired coach believes that out of the ashes hope can rise.

From the ashes we rose.

pain. *noun.* **An unpleasant sensation occurring in varying degrees of severity as a consequence of injury, disease, or emotional disorder**

Charles Dickens said he had been bent and broken, but—he hoped—into a better shape. We all come up against the problem of pain at some time or other in our lives, but hopefully, like Dickens, we survive the pain and come out in better shape than when we started. This chapter helps us learn about the benefits of pain as we grow into the person God wants us to be.

Synopsis

We Are Marshall stars Matthew McConaughey as Jack Lengyel, the optimistic newly recruited head coach who leads Marshall University from tragedy to triumph after the shattering loss of all but four varsity football players. He takes a position nobody else wants, for a team nobody else believes in. Together, they pull off a miracle nobody can stop talking about.

Like so many small towns throughout America, Huntington, West Virginia, lives and breathes college football. The time-honored tradition of young men suffering physical pain while coaches, fans, faculty, and townspeople cheer them on to victory nearly came to a halt on November 14, 1970. After a loss to East Carolina University, seventy-five Marshall University football players, coaching staff, and supporters died in the tragic crash of Southern Airways Flight 932.

In a tight-knit town where college football is revered, there is probably not one person in Huntington immune to the grief that blankets the community upon hearing the news. So great is their heartbreak that university president Donald Dedmon (David Strathairn) contemplates suspending the football program for the season—perhaps indefinitely.

President Dedmon informs the four remaining players that he will be asking the board to suspend the football program, though their scholarships will be honored. Impassioned team captain Nate Ruffin (Anthony Mackie), who struggles with the guilt of being alive simply because an injured shoulder kept him from traveling with the team, organizes a rally of virtually the entire student body, prompting President Dedmon to change his mind.

The board agrees to rebuild the team despite misgivings from some of the town's prominent citizens, including Paul Griffen (Ian McShane), whose son was among the casualties. Two glaring problems remain, however: no head coach and only four players. After being turned down by every available coach he calls, Dedmon is forced to settle for Jack Lengyel, an unknown entity.

The newly minted coach lures back a reluctant Red Dawson (Matthew Fox), the only living member of the previous staff. Red, however, is haunted by survivor's guilt. He is alive because he elected to drive so another staff member could get home for his granddaughter's recital.

Prior to the loss of the football team, the National Collegiate Athletic Association (NCAA) mandate stated that freshmen athletes could not play on the varsity squad. Lengyel convinces Dedmon, who successfully petitions the NCAA to grant freshmen eligibility to help Marshall field a team. Using players from the junior varsity squad, incoming freshmen, and players from other sports, Lengyel and Dawson build a team for the 1971 season.

Less than a year after the plane crash, the Thundering Herd of Marshall would defy overwhelming odds by marching onto the gridiron for the school's first game since that heart-breaking day. That season, it didn't matter whether Marshall won, or lost, or how well they played the game. All that mattered was that they played.

Annie Cantrel (Kate Mara) narrates the film showing vulnerability as the head cheerleader, who is devastated by the death of her football player fiancé. How Annie and others deal with the tragedy and pain of their overwhelming loss makes *We Are Marshall* different from most clichéd sports dramas.

In the second game of the season, on September 25, 1971, Marshall won their first game, against Xavier University. They didn't have a winning season that year. As the images of the celebratory team and fans play, a voiceover tells us that Marshall lost more football games in the 1970s than any other football team in the nation. It wasn't until 1984 that the Herd had their first winning season in twenty years.

By then what Jack Lengyel said was true. They were "like any other team in every other sport where winning is everything and nothing else matters." The Thundering Herd followed that winning season with eight conference titles, five conference bids and two national championships.

From the ashes they rose.

Chap. 7 — WE ARE MARSHALL
Study Guide, Week One, Pain

Principle Scripture
For everything there is a season, and a time for every matter under heaven; a time to weep, and a time to laugh; a time to mourn, and a time to dance. —Ecclesiastes 3:1, 4

The Pain Principle
The first words we hear in the film are those of Marshall cheerleader Annie Cantrell. "In the middle of Huntington, West Virginia, there's a river. Next to this river there is a steel mill. And next to the steel mill there is a school. In the middle of the school, there is a fountain. Each year on the exact same day, at the exact same hour, the water to this fountain is turned off. And in this moment once every year, throughout the town, throughout the school, time stands still." The reality is that time doesn't stand still, and the people of Huntington, West Virginia, and Marshall University had to move on with their lives. Those first hours, days, and months were filled with unimaginable grief at the loss of loved ones, as well as their football program. As they rediscovered the joy of football, each day became more normal.

Principle Ponderings
1. When he decided to shut down the football program, do you think President Dedmon was more concerned about the feelings of those in town who had lost loved ones or do you think it was something else?

2. People grieve in different ways. Was there one right answer as to the future of the football program?

3. Romans 12:15 teaches us to rejoice with those who rejoice and to weep with those who weep. Do you think people who experienced such a devastating loss could still rejoice with others at the football games? Do you think it helped in the healing process?

Principle Philosophies

1. Jesus died on the cross to give us eternal life. He also died to take away our pain.
2. God is bigger than any grief or sorrow that we have or will ever face.
3. Missing someone doesn't mean you can't enjoy life.

Principle Passages

1. Fresh activity is the only means of overcoming adversity.
   —Johann Wolfgang von Goethe
2. The will of God is never exactly what you expect it to be. It may seem to be much worse, but in the end it's going to be a lot better and a lot bigger. —Elisabeth Elliot
3. Find a place inside where there's joy, and the joy will burn out the pain. —Joseph Campbell

Principle Possibilities

1. Saying goodbye doesn't mean you stop loving someone or that their memory can ever be replaced. How effective have you been at moving on with life after a significant loss?
2. Do you believe that Romans 8:28 is applicable to you in every situation in your life? If not, what will it take to believe it?
3. What interests and dreams have you put off because of pain in your life? Will pursuing them help you to move forward?

Principle Point ❧

In 2004 Fairfield Stadium, where the Marshall football team played their home games in the 1970s, was demolished. Herndon Stadium in Atlanta was used as the stand-in for Fairfield Stadium.

Chap. 7 — WE ARE MARSHALL
Study Guide, Week Two, Pain

Principle Scripture

Blessed are those who mourn, for they shall be comforted.

—Matthew 5:4

The Pain Principle

Pain is an inevitable part of life. We know that physical pain such as broken bones, recovering from surgery, or getting over an illness takes a prescribed amount of time. Emotional pain takes time to heal, too, and there is no set timetable. In an emotional scene from *We Are Marshall* President Dedmon asks the newly hired coach why he chose to move his family to a new town to take a job no one else wanted. Coach Lengyel explains that when he heard about the challenge of rebuilding an entire football program after the devastating crash, he thought about his wife and three young children. He could not imagine the emotional pain of losing his entire family and then he thought about a team, and a school, and a town where that pain was multiplied beyond measure. How could he not use his ability to help heal a town?

Principle Ponderings

1. How do you think the remaining Marshall players, coaches, and staff who were not on the plane felt being the only survivors of the program?

2. Paul Griffith and Nate Ruffin had opposing views on starting up the football program. Why did Griffith feel it was too soon? Why did Nate think it should happen? Do you think the town was equally divided?

3. Do you think having an outsider as the new coach helped the healing process more than if Red Dawson had taken the job?

Principle Philosophies

1. We can never make a brand new start, but we can make a new ending.
2. Even pain doesn't make life stand still.
3. God allows your pain so that the empathy and compassion you learn can help someone else.

Principle Passages

1. God whispers to us in our pleasures, speaks in our conscience, but shouts in our pains: it is his megaphone to rouse a deaf world. —C. S. Lewis
2. Life's unfairness is not irrevocable; we can help balance the scales for others, if not always for ourselves
   —Hubert Humphrey
3. Pain is never permanent. —Teresa of Avila

Principle Possibilities

1. What painful situation in your past can you use to comfort someone in your present?
2. We have very little control over external forces that cause pain, but we can control the type of support systems we build to face what happens. What does your support team look like?
3. As you look at the pain of your past you have two choices: one, to mourn what used to be, the other to use the pain to be the person God means you to be. What choice are you making?

Principle Point ෴

Thousands of blow-up dummies and Computer Graphics extras joined hundreds of local extras in the large stadium scenes to make a sellout out crowd.

Chap, 7 — WE ARE MARSHALL
Study Guide, Week Three, Pain

Principle Scripture

He will wipe away every tear from their eyes, and death shall be no more, neither shall there be mourning nor crying nor pain any more, for the former things have passed away.

—REVELATION 21:4

The Pain Principle

Sometimes there are no answers and asking the question nearly destroyed Nate with guilt. Before the first game team captain Nate Ruffin wrongly believes the burden of success rests on his injured shoulders. With tears streaming down his face he pleads with the coach to let him play despite the injury. He cries, "Coach, that... was my team. They left it in my hands." Lengyel gently answers with great wisdom, "No. No, they did not. They just left." No platitudes, no pretending to know why.

Principle Ponderings

1. Red Dawson and Nate Ruffin each struggled with guilt in addition to their grief. How did their guilt differ in each case?

2. Some people might call their guilt unreasonable. Do you think it was? What would you have said or done to help them both feel less guilty?

3. At the end of the movie we learn that Red never coached again after that first season. Why do you think he quit coaching?

Principle Philosophies

1. Guilt can be regret for what we have done or what we have failed to do.

2. Don't let yesterday's guilt take away today's joy.

3. At some point guilt is a luxury we can't afford.

Principle Passages
1. How unhappy is he who cannot forgive himself.
   —Publilius Syrus
2. The worst guilt is to accept an unearned guilt
   —Ayn Rand
3. Whether we're prepared or not, life has a habit of thrusting situations upon us. —Lucille Ball

Principle Possibilities
1. Someone once suggested that we should get off the cross because someone else needs the wood. What does that mean? Is there a cross you have been on for far too long?
2. Is there someone who is overwhelmed with guilt because you have not forgiven them? Do you need to ask forgiveness from someone so you can let go of your guilt?
3. When was the last time you prayed about the guilt you are experiencing?

Principle Point ꙮ
At the movie premieres in Huntington, West Virginia, and Hollywood they used a green carpet the same color as Marshall University's school color rather than the traditional red carpet.

Chap. 7 — WE ARE MARSHALL
Study Guide, Week Four

Principle Scripture
Fear not, for I am with you, be not dismayed, for I am your God; I will strengthen you, I will help you, I will uphold you with my victorious right hand. —Isaiah 41:10

The Pain Principle

Before the first game of the new season, Lengyel finds Dawson in an empty church. Dawson is wondering whether taking to the field with little chance of winning is honoring the dead or mocking them. Lengyel helps Dawson to look at the bigger picture. "One day," explains Lengyel, "not today, not tomorrow, not this season, probably not next season either but one day, you and I are gonna wake up and suddenly we're gonna be like every other team in every other sport where winning is everything and nothing else matters. And when that day comes, well that's, that's when we'll honor them."

Principle Ponderings

1. Coach Lengyel argues that "it isn't whether we win or lose—or even how we play the game. All that matters is that we play the game." Do you agree? Is it the same with life?

2. What techniques did Coach Lengyel have to employ to build the first Marshall team? What did he do to learn how to run the veer offense? What made him willing to try new and unorthodox things?

3. When Marshall wins their first game, Lengyel gives President Dedmon the game ball even though the president has just been fired. Why do you think the coach thought Dedmon should receive the ball? Do you think he deserved it?

Principle Philosophies

1. Every success begins with a decision to succeed.

2. Sometimes asking for help is all that is needed.

3. Don't be afraid to try new things no matter what others think.

WE ARE MARSHALL

Principle Passages

1. The world is full of suffering; it is also full of overcoming it. —Helen Keller
2. It is not right to say that all suffering perfects. It only perfects one type of person . . . the one who accepts the call of God in Christ Jesus. —Oswald Chambers
3. Anyone who has never made a mistake has never tried anything new. —Albert Einstein

Principle Possibilities

1. Annie and her fiancé Chris had been planning a move to California before his death. Only after the first season does she leave town to start her life. What have you been putting off doing? Why?
2. In the movie we learn that Coach Lengyel wasn't the best guy for the job, but he was the only one willing to take it. Is there a job that only you can do? What's stopping you from doing it?
3. Marshall lost more football games in the 1970s than any other football team in the nation. Are you willing to be that patient in achieving your goals?

Principle Point ❧

The real-life Red Dawson has a cameo role as the head coach of Morehead State.

PRAYING HANDS

Pain nourishes courage. You can't be brave if you've only had wonderful things happen to you. — Mary Tyler Moore

Around the year 1490, there were two young friends, Albrecht Dürer and Franz Königstein, both very poor, struggling artists, so poor that they had to work to support themselves while they studied.

As eager as they both were to perfect their craft, their work took so much of their time that there were few moments left for art. Finally, they agreed to a plan. If one of them could study exclusively, he would surely become successful. The one who achieved such fame would then pay for the other friend to study. After drawing lots, Albrect began his education while Franz supported them both.

Albrect went off to the cities of Europe to learn. As predicted, he did attain that elusive success and, as promised, went back to keep his vow to Franz. It was when Albrecht returned home to Franz that he saw the enormous cost his friend had paid.

While Albrect had spent his time learning and drawing, Franz had done manual labor to provide for him. By doing such painful work his fingers had become stiff and gnarled; his artists' hands were ruined for life. But although his dreams would never be realized, he was not bitter. Instead, he rejoiced at all his friend had achieved.

One day, greatly saddened that his friend Franz could no longer paint because of his ruined hands, Albrecht came to his friend and found him kneeling, with his twisted hands positioned in prayer. Despite the pain and disappointment Franz was praying for his friend, though he himself could no longer be an artist. His pain and sacrificial love for his friend helped to create one of the most beautiful and meaningful pieces of art ever drawn.

Albrecht Dürer sketched the folded hands of his faithful friend and later completed his greatest masterpiece, "The Praying Hands."

—EIGHT—

Principle Scripture

Let all bitterness and wrath and anger and clamor and slander be put away from you, with all malice, and be kind to one another, tender-hearted, forgiving one another, as God in Christ forgave you. —EPHESIANS 4:31–32

The Transformative Power of
PARDON

The Harimaya Bridge

THE IMPOSSIBILITY OF FORGIVENESS

> *Judge not, and you will not be judged;*
> *condemn not, and you will not*
> *be condemned; forgive,*
> *and you will be forgiven.*
> —LUKE 6:37

Living what we preach can be impossible even when you are a renowned speaker and evangelist. Corrie ten Boom was a Dutch Christian who, with her father and other family members, helped many Jews escape the Nazi Holocaust during World War II. After being turned in by a Dutch informant, the ten Boom family was arrested and sent to Scheveningen prison, where her father died ten days after his arrest. One sister, brother, and nephew were all released, but Corrie and her sister, Betsie, were eventually transported to Ravensbrück concentration camp in Germany, where Betsie grew weaker and died. Due to a clerical error Corrie was released on December 28, 1944, just a week before all of the female prisoners her age were killed.

After the war Corrie traveled around the world, sharing her story and encouraging forgiveness. Before she died her sister told her, "There is no pit so deep that God's love is not deeper still," but it wasn't until 1947 that she came to understand the depths of God's love.

In her book *The Hiding Place*, Corrie tells of coming face-to-face with one of the Ravensbrück guards. She describes his uniform, her shame of being paraded naked in front of this man, her frail sister walking in front of her.

Though he did not recognize Corrie, after hearing her mention Ravensbrück the man shared that he had worked there but had since become a Christian. "I know that God has forgiven me for the cruel things I did there, but I would like to hear it from your lips as well. Fraulein"... his hand came out... "will you forgive me?"

She describes feeling as if she stood for hours staring at the man's outstretched hand. She realized that God's conditional forgiveness stresses the importance of our forgiving those who have wronged us. "Forgiveness is an act of the will, and the will can function regardless of the temperature of the heart. Jesus, help me!" she prayed silently. "I can lift my hand, I can do that much. You supply the feeling."

With not a shred of forgiveness in her heart Corrie thrust her hand into his. "The current started in my shoulder, raced down my arm, sprang into our joined hands. And then this healing warmth seemed to flood my whole being, bringing tears to my eyes. "I forgive you, brother!" I cried. "With all my heart!"

The need to forgive is universal. In the *The Harimaya Bridge* Japan is used as a stunning backdrop for forgiveness and redemption. Daniel Holder is imprisoned by grief and decades old anger and prejudice. Like Corrie, Daniel learns to forgive and in this beautifully filmed movie we see anger and bitterness slowly replaced by pardon and love.

THE HARIMAYA BRIDGE

*A journey across the bridge
into forgiveness and love*

par•don. *noun.* **Allowance or forgiveness for an offense or a discourtesy**

Whether you call it pardon or forgiveness it is still one of the most difficult things to do whether it applies to others or to our own self. Truer words were never spoken on the subject than those by Saint Francis of Assisi when he said, "Where there is injury let me sow pardon."

Synopsis

In *The Harimaya Bridge,* Ben Guillory plays retired photographer Daniel Holder, an African American father whose son, Mickey, died in a traffic accident while he was teaching English in Japan. Daniel's father was in a Japanese POW camp during World War II, and, as he says, it didn't end well. His entire life he has hated the Japanese, and now his only son has died in the country that has nothing but negative connotations for him.

As the story unfolds Daniel decides that someone must travel to Kochi Prefecture in rural Japan, where his son taught, to bring Mickey's paintings back home to San Francisco. Daniel's brother Joseph (Danny Glover) suggests that Daniel himself make the trek to Japan to accomplish his mission. When no one else will go for him, he realizes that if he wants the paintings he thinks of as rightfully his, he will have to make the journey.

The majority of *The Harimaya Bridge* takes place in Japan, and most of the characters do not speak English. This, along with a myriad of cultural differences, poses challenges for Daniel. In the beginning of his odyssey, we have yet to unravel the complexities of his back story so we have no clue as to why he carries such resentment toward Japan. We also don't have a complete picture of how his relationship with his son disintegrated. In Daniel we find someone cold and bad mannered. Because of his complete disregard for his Japanese hosts and their culture we do not like him, let alone sympathize with his position.

After the long trip, Daniel stands confused at the airport trying to figure out how to get to the apartment offered to him by a teacher at Mickey's school. Before he attempts to find transportation, county school office employees Yuiko Hara (Misa Shimuzu,) Kunji Inoue (Hajime Yamazaki), and Saita Nakayama (Misono) arrive. This is the first of many kindnesses shown to Daniel, and yet he remains taciturn to the point of rudeness. Yukio speaks English quite well and shows Daniel every courtesy. He in turn is scathingly impolite. He refuses to remove his shoes in the apartment. When he finally does take them off he kicks them carelessly rather than placing them neatly as a sign of respect as the others do.

Daniel has a list he found in Mickey's belongings of all the paintings given as gifts, along with the names of the recipients. He wants to take every piece of art home to San Francisco so this Japanese chapter can be closed. The Japanese treasure gifts, so when asked to collect the paintings, Yukio, Kunji, and Saita do not know how to respond. Taking back a gift is incredibly disrespectful, and though they agree to make calls on his behalf, it is obvious they are uncomfortable with the task.

Daniel asks especially about Mickey's friend Noriko and is told she resigned shortly after Mickey's death and they have no idea of her whereabouts. When pressed, Kunji calls her parents and is told after harsh words that they too do not know where she is living. Through flashbacks, stories, and a visit to Mickey's school, we learn that he enjoyed teaching English and was liked and respected by both students and co-workers. When Daniel visits the school he finds a painting Mickey has given to them surrounded by pictures and letters the students have left as a tribute to their beloved teacher. The principal is visibly shocked when he learns of Daniel's plan to take Mickey's painting to America.

In addition to teaching English, Mickey also taught art classes. While at the school Daniel meets Mickey's favorite student, a special needs girl, who presents him with a number of pictures she drew of Mickey, including one of a young Japanese woman holding a brown baby.

Daniel tricks the irrepressible Saita into taking him to Noriko Kubo's (Saki Takaoka) family home. Noriko's father is furious when he opens the door and finds a man who could only be Mickey's father. He files a complaint with the county office and Saita is fired.

Putting the pieces together, Daniel's focus switches from the artwork to a possible grandchild. Yukio arranges a meeting with Emi, the young special needs artist, and her teacher. After a gentle talk with her they learn where Noriko is living. Emi confirms that there is a baby and Yukio and Daniel go to her village to find Noriko and her daughter. Seeing his only granddaughter gives Daniel hope and he urges Noriko not to give her daughter up for adoption as she is considering. Raising a child alone is hard enough, but even more difficult with a mixed-race child in Japan.

Yukio takes Daniel to the town's small museum where he discovers Mickey's artwork displayed. Yukio explains that when Mickey died the people who had received them as gifts donated them to the museum to create a permanent exhibit.

Daniel shares with Yukio about Mickey's passion for his art and a pivotal trip to New York when, as a young child, he vowed that one day his work would be displayed in a museum. In the end, seeing his son's dream come to fruition in the small museum is of much greater importance than retrieving the paintings.

Throughout *The Harimaya Bridge* there are scenes showing Daniel holding or reading snippets from the last letter he sent to Mickey in Japan. After meeting his daughter-in-law and granddaughter, and seeing his son's paintings on display, the rest of the letter is revealed. As Daniel reads the hurtful comments he wrote to his only son we see a flashback of Mickey's tearful reaction to his father's words. Only by coming to terms with the past can Daniel forgive himself and move forward.

Further conversations with Noriko and Yukio help him to realize that both women experienced discrimination because of the men they loved. In both cases their families disapproved of their choices resulting in shame and estrangement. Daniel realizes that the way he alienated his own son for going to Japan was just like the way Noriko's family alienated her for her relationship and marriage to Mickey.

The movie begins with an artist painting on a canvas. The picture of a couple on a bridge emerges, but it's not until late in the film that we understand the significance of the painting. According to legend, while standing on the Harimaya Bridge, a Shinto priest gave his beloved a hairpin as a sign of his love. They were banished separately because their love was forbidden. A replica of the bridge is reproduced in Kochi, and it is that scene represented in Mickey's painting.

This legend of forbidden love is a parallel for the relationship between Mickey and Noriko, two people from completely different backgrounds who are drawn together by love. Their relationship becomes a bridge between their worlds.

That bridge ultimately becomes a way for Daniel to put to rest his anger and resentment toward his son and the Japanese people. He decides that if the only way to have an ongoing presence in his granddaughter Mariya's life is to stay in Japan, then he will move to Japan. Coming from America to visit him, his family sees a new, unburdened man with a thriving photography business and a new family, including Noriko's parents, who have also crossed the bridge. He has even hired Saita, who had lost her job earlier, as his assistant.

The Harimaya Bridge is a story about acceptance and forgiveness—life-changing lessons for us all to learn and live by.

Chap. 8 — THE HARIMAYA BRIDGE
Study Guide, Week One, Pardon

Principle Scripture

A man of quick temper acts foolishly, but a man of discretion is patient. —Proverbs 14:17

The Pardon Principle

Daniel Holder is an angry man. His father died in a Japanese prisoner of war camp during World War II, and for decades he has held on to bitterness and prejudice. Quiet by nature, he has never discussed his father's death with his family, including his younger brother. Now he is in Japan on a mission that will change everything. Daniel has no interest in honoring customs different from his, such as removing his shoes upon entering a building, and seems almost intent on being rude. Over and over his hosts are unfailingly kind to him in the face of his bad behavior. A letter he found in his son's belongings gives us a clue as to who is most in need of forgiveness. By the end of the movie we know that Daniel has learned that he must forgive the unpardonable because Christ pardoned him.

Principle Ponderings

1. Why did Daniel decide to try to retrieve his son's artwork, even though it meant going there himself? Do you think it was out of anger or to help him through the grieving process?

2. How did Mickey betray his father? What further betrayal do we learn of once he is in Japan?

3. Daniel came to this country with an intense hatred of all Japan and that anger spilled over into his dealings with everyone. How did Mickey's friends and co-workers react to Daniel's rude behavior?

Principle Philosophies

1. Anger becomes sin when God's plan is distorted.
2. Understanding why people are angry doesn't justify their bad behavior. It might, however, be an open door to helping them resolve their anger and move on.
3. You are the person most hurt by your anger.

Principle Passages

1. Speak when you are angry—and you'll make the best speech you'll ever regret. —Laurence J. Peter
2. Anger is an acid that can do more harm to the vessel in which it is stored than to anything on which it is poured.
   —Mark Twain
3. Be angry but do not sin; do not let the sun go down on your anger, and give no opportunity to the devil.
   —Ephesians 4:26–27

Principle Possibilities

1. Colossians 3:13 says, "Bear with one another and, if anyone has a complaint against another, forgive each other; just as the Lord has forgiven you, so you also must forgive." Are there people in your life you need to forgive? Are there those who you need to ask for forgiveness?
2. Proverbs 15:1 tells us that a soft answer turns away wrath, but a harsh word stirs up anger. How do you respond to those who treat you unfairly?
3. When you are angry act, don't react. Handle your anger biblically by returning good for evil. Do not be overcome by evil, but overcome evil with good (Romans 12: 21). Are there situations when you reacted instead of acting?

What were the consequences? Do you need to build a bridge to forgiveness because of your actions?

Principle Point ॐ
Director Aaron Woolfolk was a Japanese English Teacher in Kochi Prefecture, where the movie was set.

Chap. 8 — THE HARIMAYA BRIDGE Study Guide, Week Two, Pardon

Principle Scripture
Pride goes before destruction, a haughty spirit before a fall.
—Proverbs 16:18

The Pardon Principle
When Daniel arrives in Japan he has an opportunity to learn more about Mickey's life and to come to terms with his death. Yet in the beginning of his time there he is unwilling to see anything of value in the entire country. Daniel is prideful, and that unwillingness to consider the possibility of his not being right is a huge stumbling block on his road to forgiveness. Once in Japan he is single-minded in his goal of removing Mickey's artwork from Japan. He is so intent on that goal that, knowing what he was doing is wrong, he convinces Saita to take him to Noriko's family home, getting her fired in the process. His prideful actions disappoint the principal at Mickey's school when he takes the treasured gift Mickey gave them. Pride made Daniel unable to give up his need to be right, even when he was wrong.

Principle Ponderings
1. What other example of Daniel's pride do we see?
2. Philippians 2:3 reminds us to "do nothing from selfishness or conceit, but in humility count others better than yourselves." What are examples of Daniel putting himself above others?

3. Was there ever a time when Daniel realized that he must give up his need to be right?

Principle Philosophies
1. Pride is a way of justifying one's bad behavior.
2. When proud people look down on others, they don't look up to God.
3. Pride is a way of deceiving yourself.

Principle Passages
1. Pride only breeds quarrels, but wisdom is found in those who take advice. —Proverbs 13:10
2. Proud people breed sad sorrows for themselves.
   —Emily Brontë
3. If I had only one sermon to preach it would be a sermon against pride. —G. K. Chesterton

Principle Possibilities
1. Where is pride causing a problem in your life?
2. Is pride standing in the way of giving or accepting forgiveness?
3. God alone can heal us of our pride. Have you spoken to God about a prideful situation?

Principle Point ❧Aaron Woolfolk was the first African American to direct a movie in Japan.

Chap. 8 — THE HARIMAYA BRIDGE
Study Guide, Week Three, Pardon

Principle Scripture
Blessed are the peacemakers, for they shall be called sons of God.
—Matthew 5:9

THE HARIMAYA BRIDGE

The Pardon Principle

Daniel was angry and prideful and unwilling to forgive; Yukio, his exact opposite. From her first onscreen appearance, she took on the role of a peacemaker. With her soft-spoken voice and gentle wisdom, Yukio's patience in the face of Daniel's obstinate and unkind behavior is a lesson to us all. Even when she reprimanded Daniel for what he had done she did so without going overboard. Her lack of foul words and aggressive body language speaks volumes about her character and her contentment with herself. Without Yukio this story could have ended much differently. We are called to be a "Yukio" in dealing with difficult people to help learn to forgive and be better people.

Principle Ponderings

1. When did Yukio have to reprimand Daniel? Which reprimand do you think had the most impact on Daniel? Why?
2. What qualities did Yukio possess in her dealings with Daniel, Emi, and others that you wish to emulate?
3. How did Noriko show her peaceful nature?

Principle Philosophies

1. Most people love peace, but they are not willing to be a peacemaker.
2. When we work for peace, we are following Christ's example.
3. If we respond correctly, conflict can glorify God.

Principle Passages

1. If possible, so far as it depends upon you, live peaceably with all. —ROMANS 12:8
2. A good example is the best sermon. —BEN FRANKLIN

3. Our patience will achieve more than our force.

—Edmund Burke

Principle Possibilities

1. Do you strive to be a peacemaker with difficult people?
2. Is there a situation where you need to stand back and let someone else be a peacemaker so the situation can be resolved?
3. Are there times when a reprimand is needed? How can you maintain peace while still being just?

Principle Point ✇

The actual Harimaya Bridge sits in the middle of Kochi City, Japan, and can be seen in the film.

Chap. 8 — THE HARIMAYA BRIDGE
Study Guide, Week Four

Principle Scripture

Hatred stirs up strife, but love covers all offenses.

—Proverbs 10:12

The Pardon Principle

When Daniel found out that he had a grandchild everything changed. Until then his anger, his pride, his needs were all that mattered. Daniel needed to analyze his anger and put his life back into perspective. Compounding his need to right the wrongs he had loosed with the letter he wrote to Mickey and his hatred of the Japanese was seeing a way to make Mickey's dream come true. Once he saw the paintings in the small museum he knew he could never take them back to America. Character is a long-standing habit. Thanks to his time in Japan Daniel can now develop a new character that is a blessing to himself and others.

THE HARIMAYA BRIDGE

Principle Ponderings

1. Did Daniel think of the consequences of his words before sending the final letter to Mickey?
2. Do you think Daniel was happy in his new homeland? Why or why not? Do you think his moving to Japan helped or harmed Mariya?
3. Who else benefited from Daniel moving to Japan?

Principle Philosophies

1. Forgiveness does not change the past, but it does enlarge the future.
2. People can be more forgiving than you can imagine. But you have to forgive yourself.
3. Letting go of the bitterness allows you to move on.

Principle Passages

1. He that cannot forgive others breaks the bridge over which he must pass himself; for every man has need to be forgiven. —THOMAS FULLER
2. Forgiveness is the final form of love.
   —REINHOLD NIEBUHR
3. When you haven't forgiven those who've hurt you, you turn your back against your future. When you do forgive you start walking forward. —TYLER PERRY

Principle Possibilities

1. What future are you looking forward to through the gift of forgiveness?
2. Are there toxic people in your life who need your prayers?
3. What will you do today to facilitate forgiveness?

Principle Point ✣
Danny Glover's birthday was the same night the concert scene was filmed. During the first take, when the director said "action," instead of playing the music for the scene the orchestra played Happy Birthday, followed by a cake being brought onto the set.

FORGIVEN, NOT FORGOTTEN

> *Forgiveness does not change the past,*
> *but it does enlarge the future.*
> —Paul Boese

Sixty-eight pounds. That's what twenty-two-year-old Immaculee Ilibagiza weighed after spending ninety-one days in a three-foot by four-foot bathroom during the 1994 killing spree in her homeland. Immaculee is a Tutsi, the ethnic minority in Rwanda. While home for Easter break from National University, where she was studying electrical and mechanical engineering, Hutu death squads began a three-month killing spree of Tutsis across the nation.

When the killing began, Immaculee's father believed that an Episcopalian minister three miles away would hide her even though he was a Hutu. Despite their differences the two families had been friends, and so, because he believed in the goodness of this priest, she fled to his home, clutching a rosary from her father.

She and seven other women hid in the tiny bathroom with a dresser pushed over the doorframe to hide it from view. Unable to talk for fear that Hutu soldiers on the hunt would hear them, they barely survived on scraps of food. During her ninety-one days in hiding she taught herself English using only a Bible and a dictionary. And her faith grew stronger than all of the losses combined.

When they emerged, between five hundred thousand and eight hundred thousand Tutsis were dead, including Immaculee's parents, grandparents, and three brothers. She and the others found refuge in a camp just a few miles from the pastor's home.

In her 2006 memoir, *Left to Tell: Discovering God Amid the Rwandan Holocaust,* Immaculee tells of getting an opportunity to face her family's killers. When the massacre ended, she was allowed inside the prison where Hutu militants were being detained. A guard shouted demands at the killer to tell the now-orphaned student why he had killed her family. "It was just in that moment when I saw him that my heart was heaped with compassion. It was like a ray of compassion in my heart that shocked me." She says she saw how "the evil had ruined his life like a cancer in his soul." As the man sobbed, Immaculee picked up his hand and told him, "I forgive you."

Immaculee, now an author and inspirational speaker, believes that God has a purpose for her life, to share the message of forgiveness. "I believe in the law of love. We must love each other. When you forgive, you can't believe the transformation that takes place in your heart." She adds quietly, "If I can forgive, anyone can forgive."

—NINE—

Principle Scripture
I press on toward the goal for the prize of the upward call of God in Christ Jesus. —Philippians 3:14

The Transformative Power of
THE PRIZE

Rudy

THE RELUCTANT HALL OF FAMER

> *So see every opportunity as golden,*
> *and keep your eyes on the prize—*
> *yours, not anybody else's.*
> —Roberta Flack

Curtis Martin never wanted to play football. Yet over a span of ten years the former New England Patriots and New York Jets running back broke records, eventually landing him in the Pro Football Hall of Fame.

Martin went out for football his senior year in high school because his mother wanted him to have an extracurricular activity that would keep him away from Pittsburgh's violent streets. Martin's father, an abusive alcoholic who tortured his mother, was by then absent, but the memories of his tragic home life were never far away.

A natural athlete, Martin learned to excel at a game he did not enjoy because he had his eye on a prize. Unlike most aspiring athletes, the prize Martin sought wasn't about winning or making it to the top of his game. When the Patriots drafted him in 1995 his first inclination was to say, "No thank you." That's when God stepped in.

"Curtis," explained Pastor Leroy Joseph, "look at it this way. Maybe football is just something that God is giving you to do all those wonderful things that you say you want to do for other people."

When he was twenty Martin promised God that if he made it to twenty-one, he would give his life over to his faith and "do whatever you want me to do." For the future Hall of Famer that meant football because that was a way to help people.

Unlike Martin, the protagonist in the movie *Rudy* loved everything about football and, more specifically, Notre Dame football. Rudy had his eye on the prize for a different reason yet, in the end, like Martin he too won his prize.

Winning earthly prizes is exciting, especially when in the process we can help others. But the true prize comes when our time on earth ends. Only we can win the ultimate prize, our salvation.

It's not the size of the dog in the fight;
it's the size of the fight in the dog.
—Mark Twain

prize. *noun.* **Something worth striving for; a highly desirable possession**

Grammy award winning singer Roberta Flack told us to see every opportunity as golden, and keep your eyes on the prize—yours, not anybody else's. Her statement is true in life and especially true when our time on earth is done. No one can win anyone else's salvation. Rudy is an excellent example of one man who lived all the previous eight principles in such a way that he could win the ultimate prize.

Synopsis

If you are from a town like Joliet, Illinois, and from a working-class family, the local steel mill is probably where you'll start and finish your career. Anyone who knew Daniel "Rudy" Ruettiger

(Sean Astin) knew that he wasn't college bound. His father, Daniel Sr. (Ned Beatty) works in the mill and tries to persuade Rudy that he shouldn't dream of anything more than a stable job to provide for the family that is sure to come. If it's good enough for him it should be good enough for Rudy.

But Rudy has a different dream, a dream his father unwittingly instilled in him by insisting that in the Ruettiger house they only watch Notre Dame football. Despite his dismal grades, small stature, and no money, Rudy dreams of playing football for the Fighting Irish.

When Rudy tries to go on a school-sponsored field trip to visit the Notre Dame campus, a teacher tells him that attendance is limited to those with a hope of being admitted. No one in his family is supportive of his goal, and his older brother, Frank, never misses an opportunity to ridicule him. With no other option, after graduation Rudy takes a job at a local steel mill. With a job and a serious girlfriend his only connection to Notre Dame will most likely be in front of the television.

Sometimes having even one person who champions you is enough to keep you going. For Rudy it's his childhood friend Pete, always Rudy's encouragement and inspiration for following his dream. After high school Pete joins Rudy at the mill. Four years later, on Rudy's birthday, he gives Rudy the best birthday gift he ever received—a Notre Dame letter jacket.

"You're the only one who ever took me seriously, Pete," explains Rudy after opening the gift.

"Well, you know what my dad always said," answers Pete. "Having dreams is what makes life tolerable."

When they go back to work, Pete is killed in an explosion, and Rudy realizes if not now, when? Against his father's advice he quits his job, tells his fiancée, and boards the bus to the Midwest football Mecca with a thousand dollars in his pocket.

Encouraged by Father Cavanaugh (Robert Prosky), who erroneously thinks Rudy wants to become a priest, Rudy enrolls at a nearby junior college. His hope is that at Holy Cross he can get good enough grades to transfer the following semester. Rudy manages to get a part-time job on Notre Dame's groundskeeping staff. The head groundskeeper, Fortune (Charles S. Dutton), turns a blind eye to Rudy sleeping on a cot in a small locker room and even places a key on the cot for him to find.

Rudy becomes friends with Notre Dame student and Holy Cross teaching assistant D-Bob (Jon Favreau), who suspects an underlying cause for Rudy's academic problems. Testing proves that he has dyslexia, and Rudy learns how to overcome his disability and becomes a better student. Despite ever-improving grades his family still ridicules him. To make matters worse he doesn't get into Notre Dame after his first semester. After three rejection letters he despairs of ever getting in.

"Maybe I haven't prayed enough," wonders Rudy in a conversation with Father Cavanaugh after yet another rejection letter.

"I don't think that's the problem. Praying is something we do in our time; the answers come in God's time," replies the priest.

Rudy works even harder and finally, during his final semester of transfer eligibility, Rudy is admitted to Notre Dame. When Rudy rushes home to tell his family, his father announces over the mill loudspeaker, "Hey, you guys, my son's going to Notre Dame!" Still, others in his family are less enthusiastic, and no one believes he will make the football team.

Rudy tries out as a non-scholarship player for the football team. An assistant coach warns the players that thirty-five scholarship players won't make the roster so they shouldn't get their hopes up for making the team. Rudy, determined to get a slot, works harder and shows more heart than his scholarship teammates. Although physically too small to be a varsity player, through hard work and believing that his destiny is on the field, Rudy becomes a valuable and much-loved member of the practice team.

In desperation Rudy begs Coach Parseghian for a chance to suit up for at least one game. "I have this wish to let my father watch one of his sons play football for the Irish, and I was wondering if I could possibly dress for one game next season?"

"Is this wish just for your father?"

"No it's for everyone who told me that being a Notre Dame football player would be impossible. My brothers, the guys I work with at the mill—they can't come to practice and see that I am a part of this team."

With a sigh the coach agrees. "You deserve it. You will dress for one game next season."

It appears that Rudy's dream of running onto the field will not happen when Parseghian steps down as coach following the 1974 season. Coach Dan Devine succeeds him and decides against giving Rudy a chance to appear at a home game.

In a fit of frustration Rudy decides to quit the team. Fortune, who showed his belief by giving Rudy a job, a place to stay, and friendship, gives him a much-needed pep talk. "You're five foot nothin', a hundred and nothin', and you have barely a speck of athletic ability. And you hung in there with the best college football players in the land for two years. And you're gonna walk outta here with a degree from the University of Notre Dame. In this life, you don't have to prove nothin' to nobody but yourself. And after what you've gone through, if you haven't done that by now, it ain't gonna never happen. Now go on back."

Taking Fortune's words to heart Rudy returns to the team for the rest of the season. When Coach Devine still refuses to allow Rudy to play for the final game, the team captain and every senior laid their jerseys on Devine's desk, each requesting that Rudy be allowed to dress in their place. Devine relents and lets Rudy suit up for the final home game, against Georgia Tech.

In one of the greatest movie football scenes ever, Rudy leads the team out of the tunnel onto the playing field. Near the end of the game Notre Dame has a commanding lead and Devine sends all the seniors to the field, but refuses to let Rudy play. From the Notre Dame bench someone starts a "Rudy!" chant that soon echoes throughout the stadium. Devine finally lets

Rudy enter the field with the defensive team on the final kickoff. He stays in for the final play of the game, sacks the opposing quarterback, and is carried off on the shoulders of his teammates.

Chap. 9 — RUDY
Study Guide, Week One, The Prize

Principle Scripture
What then shall we say to this? If God is for us, who is against us?
—Romans 8:31

The Prize Principle
Rudy does not have the grades, the size, or the talent to play football for Notre Dame, but he does have one thing many people lack when it comes to winning their prize: belief. In fact, real life Daniel "Rudy" Ruettiger believed so much that his story should be a movie, that he hounded Hoosiers screenwriter Angelo Pizzo until he agreed to write the screenplay and worked to get it into production. That same determination is what led Rudy to his moment of glory on the football field, but it started with believing in himself.

Principle Ponderings

1. Rudy came from a town that lived and breathed Notre Dame football. What was the first indication that Rudy had aspirations of playing for Notre Dame? Did that motivation ever waver?

2. In the beginning, who was the one other person who believed that Rudy could attend and play for Notre Dame? What did his family think? Did his cadre of believers ever increase?

3. How did Rudy handle being ridiculed by teachers, family, and friends?

Principle Philosophies

1. You have to believe in yourself because ultimately everything is up to you.
2. Things will work out one way or another, but when you believe, the best way is God's way.
3. Even when you believe in yourself, remember that you can make a plan, but God will direct your steps.

Principle Passages

1. Now faith is the assurance of things hoped for, the conviction of things not seen. —Hebrews 11:11
2. People may doubt what you say but they will believe what you do. —Cass Lewis
3. Believe in yourself, and the rest will fall into place. Have faith in your own abilities, work hard, and there is nothing you cannot accomplish —Brad Henry

Principle Possibilities

1. Do you believe that God made you for a special purpose?
2. What dream or goal do you believe you can reach with God's help?
3. What is stopping you from achieving what you believe you are meant to do?

Principle Point ✦

The real Rudy had a non-speaking role as one of the fans in the stands at the end of the movie.

Chap. 9 — RUDY
Study Guide, Week Two, The Prize

Principle Scripture
Do you not know that in a race all the runners compete, but only one receives the prize? So run that you may obtain it.
—1 Corinthians 9:24

The Prize Principle
From the beginning we see that Rudy has passion. When he finally makes the football team it's not because of his size or his skill. In fact, Coach Parseghian says to Rudy that "I wish God would put your heart in some of my players' bodies." He tells Rudy's teammate who is bigger and has enough talent to have won a scholarship that "if you had a tenth of the heart of Ruettiger, you'd have made All-American by now!" Believing is good, but having the heart and passion to back it up is essential.

Principle Ponderings

1. We know Rudy was a hard worker on the football field. Where else did he show his heart?

2. Did anyone believe in him once he left home? Who do you think was his biggest support and why?

3. Once Rudy made the team he worked so hard he frustrated the other players by working so hard. Why do you think Rudy's teammates went from resenting to supporting Rudy?

Principle Philosophies

1. Be more passionate about God's power than your own abilities.

2. Don't let negative people belittle your dreams or your heart.

3. Look for support in unlikely places because God will never make you go it alone.

Principle Passages
   1. Some people succeed because they are destined to, but most people succeed because they are determined to.
   —Henry Ford
   2. No one can make you feel inferior without your consent.
   —Eleanor Roosevelt
   3. The soul of the sluggard craves, and gets nothing, while the soul of the diligent is richly supplied.
   —Proverbs 13:4

Principle Possibilities
   1. How would you rate your "heart health" when it comes to being passionate about what you believe God has called you to accomplish?
   2. Have you ever succeeded where others more gifted than you failed? How did that happen?
   3. If you ever accomplished a major goal, what did you learn? Was it worth what you went through?

Principle Point ℘
Rudy is only the second movie granted permission to film on the Notre Dame campus. The first was the 1940 *Knute Rockne: All American*.

Chap. 9 — RUDY
Study Guide, Week Three, The Prize

Principle Scripture
Let each of you look not only to his own interests, but also to the interests of others. —Philippians 2:4

The Prize Principle

Rudy, like everyone intent on winning a prize, got discouraged, but he kept pressing on despite every disappointment. He was focused on the end result, but he found time to help others even if in the beginning he volunteered because it might help him reach his goal. In fact, several times he was deceitful in how he got himself in a position to be available. None of us, including Rudy, has led a blameless life, yet God continues to forgive our sins and help us win the race.

Principle Ponderings

1. What were the obstacles that Rudy had to overcome in order to win the prize?

2. Who did Rudy help once he got to Notre Dame? Of those he helped who helped him the most?

3. Do you think Rudy felt badly about any of his actions? Which one do you think might have bothered him the most?

Principle Philosophies

1. Not every goal will be reached, but in the reaching you can become a better person.

2. No one will ever believe in you if you don't first believe in yourself.

3. Failure is only a setback if when we begin again we don't it more wisely.

Principle Passages

1. The price of victory is high, but so are the rewards.
   —Paul Bryant

2. It is for us to pray not for tasks equal to our powers, but for powers equal to our tasks, to go forward with a great

desire forever beating at the door of our hearts as we travel toward our distant goal. —Helen Keller

3. The way I see it, if you want the rainbow, you gotta put up with the rain. —Dolly Parton

Principle Possibilities

1. Have you ever been discouraged in the process of trying to complete a task? How did your faith help you overcome discouragement?
2. Do you think the end justifies the means if no one gets hurt in the process?
3. In your own life are you a "Rudy" focused on developing your heart while helping others, or do you tear others down to get what you want?

Principle Point ❧
In the scenes from the final game the jerseys of the players have names of actors and crew from the film.

Chap. 9 — RUDY
Study Guide, Week Four, The Prize

Principle Scripture
I have fought the good fight, I have finished the race, I have kept the faith. —2 Timothy 4:7

The Prize Principle
In one of the last scenes of the movie, Rudy's friend Steele stood beside him as they prepared to run out onto the field for the last game of the season. The player, who knew how hard Rudy had worked, asked, "Rudy, are you ready for this, champ?" With great enthusiasm, the pint-sized player who had done so much to be there, answered, "I've been ready for this my whole life." Since setting a goal to play for Notre Dame, Rudy had worked hard. He is a perfect example of someone who walked through

each of the previous eight principles to win his prize. He knew his purpose, was full aware of his potential, set his priorities, prayed to the God who makes all things possible, practiced relentlessly, persevered when things seemed hopeless, endured both physical and emotional pain, pardoned those who ridiculed him, and pressed on to receive his prize.

Once we have chosen heaven as our true home we need to emulate Rudy so we too can claim our prize.

Principle Pondering

1. What did Rudy accomplish or prove by finally fulfilling his dream?
2. What emotions did you feel when Rudy came running out of the tunnel, when the crowd began chanting, and when he got into the game?
3. What do you think was the best lesson Rudy learned and from whom did he learn it?

Principle Philosophies

1. Dream, believe, plan, and act. This is the recipe for accomplishing great things.
2. The races we run on earth prepare us for eternity.
3. When even you find it hard to believe in yourself, remember God always believes.

Principle Passages

1. To succeed you must first improve, to improve you must first practice, to practice you must first learn, and to learn you must fail. —Wesley Woo
2. We must accept finite disappointment, but never lose infinite hope. —Martin Luther King

3. And Jesus said to him, "If you can! All things are possible to him who believes." —Mark 9:23

Principle Possibilities

1. How does Rudy's journey to the final play of the game parallel our journey to heaven?
2. It's never too late. Is there a journey you have put off for too long?
3. Rudy influenced many people by getting into Notre Dame and actually making the team. Who is joining you on your journey to heaven?

Principle Point ෴

The real Rudy did, in fact, record a quarterback sack in his brief appearance in the game.

THE OLDEST ROOKIE

> *In order to succeed, your desire for success should be greater than your fear of failure.*
> —Bill Cosby

In 1948 at the age of forty-two, Leroy Robert "Satchel" Paige was the oldest rookie to start for a Major League Baseball team. He played for both the Cleveland Indians and the St. Louis Browns and while it was impressive to be brought on board at his advanced age, he was already a proven pitcher through his time with the Negro Leagues. Although younger than Paige, Jim Morris earned his own way into the record books by becoming the oldest rookie to enter Major League Baseball after a walk-on try-out.

The subject of the 2002 biopic *The Rookie*, Morris began playing baseball at the age of three. The family moved many times until they settled in Texas, when his father became a U.S. Navy recruiter. Though baseball was his first love, he played football because his high school did not have a baseball program. He did well in football, even helping his team to win the state championship, but he never gave up his dream of the ultimate prize: becoming a professional baseball player.

After high school Morris was picked 465th overall in the January 1982 amateur baseball draft by the New York Yankees, but he did not sign with them. A year later he was selected fourth overall and signed with the Milwaukee Brewers. After a series of arm injuries, disastrous for a pitcher, he was released in 1987, never having won the prize of moving out of the Single-A Minor Leagues. A second chance with the Chicago White Sox resulted in the same disappointing results. Morris retired and became a high school physical science teacher.

The story would have ended there had it not been for a bet Morris made to motivate his less than stellar baseball team; if they won the district championship, something that had never happened in the school's history, the thirty-five-year-old pitcher would try out for the big leagues.

They did, he did, and Morris began working to win the prize. The scout scoffed at the idea of such an old rookie, but when he heard Morris was trying out because of the promise he had made to his players, he agreed to let him pitch. During his try-out for the Tampa Bay Devil Rays Morris threw twelve consecutive pitches at ninety-eight miles per hour.

The decision to accept the Tampa offer proved difficult as Morris now had a wife, three children, and a full time teaching and coaching position. Realizing that the long dreamed of prize was once again in his reach, Morris signed a professional contract with the Devil Rays organization at the age of thirty-five. After a brief time with the Minor League Double-A Orlando Rays he moved up to the Triple-A Durham Bulls.

Finally, on September 18, 1999, Morris made his debut, striking out Royce Clayton of the Texas Rangers, on four pitches. The prize was his! His goal of pitching in the majors was finally realized.

Jim Morris played just twenty-one big-league games, all for the Tampa Bay Devil Rays in 1999 and 2000. Morris never recorded any wins or losses in any of his major league appearances, but that's not what matters. Dale Carnegie said that we should "develop success from failures." Morris failed on more than one occasion, but those failures, and his belief that he had what it took to be a major league baseball player, eventually led him to the prize.

Final Comments

And they lived happily ever after. Frank L. Baum set out to write an all-American fairy tale, and in fairy tales those are always the closing words. The reality, however, is that not every story is a fairy tale and even those that resemble fairy tales don't always end happily ever after.

The nine movies chosen for inclusion do have what could be called a happy ending, but of greater importance is what kind of ending you will have when your life on this earth is over: Hebrews 12:1–2 sums up the race we are running:

> Therefore, since we are surrounded by so great a cloud of witnesses, let us also lay aside every weight, and sin which clings so closely, and let us run with perseverance the race that is set before us, looking to Jesus the pioneer and perfecter of our faith, who for the joy that was set before him endured the cross, despising the shame, and is seated at the right hand of the throne of God.

In the movie Rudy fought for the prize of playing even a few minutes in a Notre Dame football game. Remember that the prize we strive for is finally making it to our true home, our happily ever after.

Credits

The Wizard of Oz (1939)

Metro-Goldwyn-Mayer (MGM), Judy Garland, Ray Bolger, Bert Lahr, Jack Haley, Frank Morgan, Billie Burke, Margaret Hamilton

Academy Awards: Best Music, Original Score, and Best Song, "Over the Rainbow"

Director: Victor Fleming

Screenwriter: Noel Langley (credited), L. Frank Baum (novel)

Rated: None

Run Time: 101 Minutes

Hugo (2011)

Metro-Goldwyn-Mayer (MGM), Asa Butterfield, Chloe Moretz, Ben Kingsley

Academy Awards: Eleven nominations, Five wins

Director: Martin Scorsese

Screenwriter: John Logan, Brian Selznick (book)

Rated: PG

Run Time: 126 Minutes

Mr. Holland's Opus (1995)

Hollywood Pictures, Interscope Communications, Polygram Filmed Entertainment, Richard Dreyfuss, Glenne Headly, Jay Thomas, Olivia Dukakis, William H. Macy

Academy Awards: Best actor nomination

Director: Stephen Herek

Screenwriter: Patrick Seane Duncan

Rated: PG-13 (for mild language)

Run Time: 143 Minutes

Lilies of the Field (1963)

Rainbow Production Company, Sidney Poitier, Lilia Skala
Academy Awards: Five nominations, One win
Director: Ralph Nelson
Screenwriter: James Poe (screenwriter), William E. Barrett (novel)
Rated: No Rating
Run Time: 94 Minutes

Akeelah and the Bee (2006)

Lions Gate Films, Keke Palmer, Angela Basset, Laurence Fishburne
Academy Awards: None
Director: Doug Atchison
Screenwriter: Doug Atchison
Rated: PG
Run Time: 112 Minutes

Under the Same Moon (2008)
(Spanish and English with Subtitles)

Creando Films, Fidecene, Potomac Pictures, Adrian Alonso, Kate del Castillo, Eugenio Derbez
Academy Awards: None
Director: Patricia Riggen
Screenwriter: Ligiah Villalobos
Rated: PG-13 l
Run time: 196 Minutes

CREDITS

We Are Marshall (2006)
Warner Bros. Pictures, Thunder Road Pictures, Legendary Pictures, Matthew McConaughey, Matthew Fox, Anthony Mackie, David Strathairn

Academy Awards: None

Director: McG

Screenwriter: Jamie Linden, Cory Helms (story)

Rated: PG

Run Time: 131 Minutes

The Harimaya Bridge (2009)
Japanese and English with subtitles)

Eleven Arts, Laterna, Booster Project, Bennett Guillory, Danny Glover, Saki Takaoka, Misa Shimizu

Academy Awards: None

Director: Aaron Woolfolk

Screenwriter: Aaron Woolfolk

Rated: PG

Run Time: 120 Minutes

Rudy (1993)
TriStar Pictures, Sean Astin, Jon Favreau, Ned Beatty

Academy Awards: None

Director: David Anspaugh

Screenwriter: Angelo Pizzo

Rated: PG

Run Time: 114 Minutes